SPEAK

LIKE A PRO

Everything you need to know to survive your next speaking gig!

****

Phil Tasci

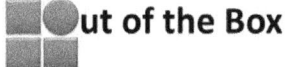

Out of the Box Publishing

Toronto

2017

Copyright © 2017 Philippe Tasci

Copyright © 2017 Out of the Box Publishing

All Rights Reserved. No part of this publication may be reproduced, stored in a retrieval system, or transmitted, in any form or in any means – by electronic, mechanical, photocopying, recording or otherwise – without prior written permission.

Published by:

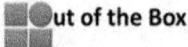 ut of the Box

Out of the Box Publishing
140 Sorauren Avenue, Suite 100, Toronto ON Canada M6R 2E5

ISBN: 978-0-9959562-0-9

Publisher: Out of the Box Publishing
Printed by: CreateSpace, Charleston SC
Cover Design: Les Solot
Photograph: Michael Lafond
Editor: Ahsan Moghul

www.philtasci.com

For

Misbah, Zohra and Zeba

Table of Contents

Preface	1
Part 1 – Content	9
Black on White	9
The Blinking Cursor	13
Before You Get Started	16
Who is Your Intended Audience?	18
Right Language, Right Audience	20
What Do They Need to Hear?	22
Where Are You Speaking?	24
Why Are You Speaking?	27
When Are You Speaking?	28
Let's Get Started…	32
The Message	32
Cut the Crap	33
Stories	36
Using Facts and Figures	41
Part 2 – Structure	47
Simple and Effective Structure	50
Creating Connection	52
Begin with a Bang	54
Tell'em What You're Going to Tell'em	56
Tell'em	57
The Rule of Three	58
A Few Good Words	59
The Roadmap	61
Making your Point	63
Facts	64
Compare and Contrast	65
Analogies and Metaphors	66
Stories	66

Quotes	68
Questions	70
A final Word on Tools	72
The Recap and Transition	73
Call to Action	75
Tell Them What You Told Them	77

Part 3 – **Delivery** — 81

Gestures	82
Eye Contact	84
A Passing Glance	86
Speak to One, Connect to All	86
The Pregnant Pause	89
Got a Question	90
Deep Thoughts	91
Never Step on Laughter	92
Rhythm, Rate, Pitch and Projection	93
Rhythm	93
Rate	95
Pitch	97
Projection	98
The Stage	100
A Measuring Stick	102
It's All About Time	102
Staging the Scene	103
Staging Points	104
Place of Power	105
Setbacks and Moving Forward	106
Moving with Purpose	107
Use the Entire Stage	109
A Few More Words on Delivery	110
Be Yourself	111
Record Yourself	113
Create a Multi-Sensory Experience	114
Dialogue Between Characters	115
Audience Involvement	118
Props, Flip Charts, and PowerPoint	120
Can I Get Some Props?	121
Flip Charts	124

PowerPoint and Projection	127
Nerves	133
A Few Final Words	137
Appendix	141

Preface

Speech is power: speech is to persuade, to convert, to compel.

-Ralph Waldo Emerson

At various times throughout our lives, we may be called upon by someone we know or love to "say a few words" to capture a moment or the spirit and essence of an event. It might be at a wedding, or a funeral, a work function or boardroom meeting, or perhaps at a celebration or party. However, regardless of what the event might be, when most people are called upon to speak publicly, they simply wish the ground would open up and swallow them whole. Public speaking has a tendency to make us feel more than a little nervous. Yet few skills will do more for you and your career than the ability to speak like a pro. Look at all those individuals who hold the key leadership positions in our society – whether in Business, the Arts, Academia or Religion – isn't it true that they all display a superior ability, comfort and confidence when speaking in public? The correlation between superior speaking skills and personal and professional success is plain for all to see. Why then is it so hard for us to find confidence in our own voices? For me and for many of you, the answer lies in our childhoods.

When I was about eight years old, my grade three teacher, (I'll leave her name out to protect the innocent), "called on me" to address my class. I thought I was going to die; I hoped that I would die. I was disappointed that I didn't die. In short, I was petrified. I had never spoken before a group of people and I had no idea what to say or do – I was at my wits end. My throat got incredibly dry while all the places on my body that should have been dry were getting sweatier by the second. I was a mess. My knees were shaking uncontrollably and I thought that I was going to be sick. I opened my mouth and tried to speak but no sound came out. Then, as if in a nightmare, the entire class, including my teacher, began to laugh loudly. It is one of the most embarrassing moments of my life to this day. Standing in front of a gaggle of giggles, I wished with all my heart that the ground would just swallow me up whole. It didn't.

That experience left a deep indelible mark on me. It was one of those terrible and traumatic memories that over time become barriers to your full development. For me it was an unfortunate and unforgettable lesson; avoid public speaking at all cost and so never let that trauma be repeated. But mine was hardly an uncommon or singular occurrence, over the years I've had so many people confide in me about some similar tragic saga or public humiliation that likewise silenced them. Over time these traumatic memories morph and mutate into the self-perpetuating fear of speaking in public.

Consequently I've come to realize that for far too many, these are the painful memories that haunt them and the consequent barriers that must be overcome. These memories, sometimes half-forgotten in our past, tell us how we should feel about public speaking. Like me, they'd rather be dead than ever have to face another audience again.

The fear of public speaking is the number one fear in the world; the second being the fear of dying. I guess that the third must be the fear of dying while speaking in public! This statistic exposes a profound vulnerability that many of us feel - a deep fear and apprehension of speaking in front of others - but to be more afraid of public speaking than death, that's crazy. Yet I totally get it because I too used to feel that way. Just the thought of it used to make me nervous and nauseous. And then sometimes life throws you a curve ball that forces you out of your stance and gets you stretching yourself beyond what you thought was possible.

For me that curve ball came years ago when my father passed away. For reasons that baffled me at the time, my family had asked me to deliver his eulogy at the funeral. Sometimes others see something in you that you can't see in yourself, and I now know that they saw that I could and would do him honour. They believed in me and so they imparted this great responsibility on me. In that devastatingly grief stricken moment, with all the emotional rawness of it, I thankfully had the presence of mind to know that I'd never forgive myself if I didn't give him a proper farewell, tell him how I felt about him and how much I would miss his smile, his voice, and his stories. That day, for only the second time in my life, I addressed a live audience. Twenty five years had passed since my grade three humiliations, yet on some emotional level it was as though it was just yesterday that I was standing in front of that class with everyone grotesquely laughing at me. I pushed through the fear.

Delivering my dad's eulogy was one of the most difficult and yet strangely, one of the most gratifying things I've ever reluctantly chosen to do. That day, speaking from the pulpit, riddled with fear, represents one of my proudest moments and one of the best decisions I've ever made.

Looking back on it now, it wasn't just the fact that I was speaking in front of dozens of people that terrified me; it was also the responsibility I felt in trying to find and structure the right words that would honour the memory and legacy of my dad's life. In a state of near detachment, as if I was in a dream or daze, I somehow got through it even though I was chocked up and fighting back tears throughout much of the speech.

In facing my fear of public speaking, I realized that delivering a speech, one that is a true reflection of your thoughts and ideas is one of the most powerful and gratifying gifts that we humans are granted. I was, and I continue to be, so incredibly grateful to my family for giving me the privilege and opportunity to celebrate my father's life and legacy by giving him the proper send-off that he so very much deserved.

Through this experience, I discovered the key lesson that the ability to move others with our words is a very powerful force. Whether it is to persuade, inspire, entertain or inform an audience, a well-crafted and well delivered speech is truly a wondrous thing to behold, and even more so, when we are blessed to be present for its live delivery. We are, each one of us, endowed with the mostly untapped power and privilege to utter the inspired words of our inner imaginings. When we choose our words carefully and convey our deepest passion, whatever that might be, those very words may end up being reflected upon or even remembered throughout history. Words have power. Whether they are simply recalled and repeated by our own families, or whether those very words you chose filter through and resonate through your business dealings, spiritual convictions, or your social communities, public speaking has the power to move others. It is a gift that everyone must develop.

Consider all the great heroes and legendary figures of our collective past, they are often remembered precisely because of the wisdom and insight of their words; words that continue to inspire in their posterity. Great speeches have emboldened soldiers as they face the horrors and potential death of the battlefield; Speeches have painted the brave new visions of what our world might aspire to be; and speeches have pronounced the concrete convictions and yearning of the poetic heart and soul. Great words and profound speeches, these have been etched into the bedrock of the collective conscience of the entire human race. This is the awesome potential and power of well-spoken words - a power that you have within you.

Choosing your words and your message well will only get you part of the way there; for a speech to be successful it must also be well-structured, allowing the message to resonate in the hearts and minds of the audience. A well-organized structure clears away any confusion giving clarity to your core message and it further aids in organizing your supporting points and proof. The design and structure of your speech must be congruent to your premise, coordinated and appropriate for the effective conveyance of your message as intended.

Public speaking is an audio visual art form, we tend to put all our focus on the concepts and language that we use, however how we say it is just as important as what we say. Delivery is the dynamo of every presentation – the sizzle in the steak. How we choose to say what we say – all the non-verbal communicators such as effective eye contact and hand gestures - is the magic that ties everything that we say into a powerful and potent package. Delivery, just as much as content and structure must be purposefully designed to successfully achieve the effective communication of our thoughts and ideas. Great dynamic delivery is quintessential to drawing your audiences in, so they can access your speech on both an emotional and a cognitive level.

Your effective delivery is, in essence, what sanctions you as "The Speaker". It allows you to come across as much more trustworthy, believable, and more likable. It's the magic that allows you to connect with and convince your audience, it's what gets your words to embolden them into action, and it can even empower them to take charge of their lives – in short great delivery is where all the elements of a speech come together and synchronize so that your message can materialize in the audience's mind.

Sadly, for too many would be speakers, this is precisely where the trouble lies; their delivery is flat. Many are simply petrified of an audience; be they family, friends or colleagues. It is so easy to become paralyzed by the fear of potential ridicule or that we will suffer some terrible embarrassment. We think: what if I freeze? What if I screw up? What if I'm boring, monotone or just totally lame? Just like in so many other areas of our lives, we are the very barriers to our own success as we succumb to the terrible and debilitating monster of self-doubt.

We owe it to ourselves, each and every one of us, to find and express our individual voice – that special gift we have been endowed with. So let me assure you, as has been said in countless different ways and at countless different times, "the only thing we have to fear is fear itself"[1]. Simply put; fear must first be confronted if it is ever to be conquered. Understanding your fears, having strategies for their defeat and building personal resilience, shifts the odds greatly in our favor. With appropriate help, sound preparation, and adequate practice you too can rise up and speak from the platform with confidence, poise, and even eloquence just like a pro!

Imagine what having these skills can do for your career, your business, your network and net worth. Leaders and experts are increasingly being invited to speak at events such as conferences, special events, business meetings or even TED talks. Speaking is also one of the best self-promotional marketing tools out there, one that more and more professionals and entrepreneurs are choosing to develop seeing a clear parallel to their business and personal success.

This book will be your life support when you think you might be sinking under the fear or stress of speaking. Remember that you are not alone - I am here beside you to guide you through to your success. Within the pages of this book are all the tools you will ever need to survive any audience and thrive at your next speaking engagement or event, whatever it may be. The truth is that there are so many important and essential tips, tools and techniques in this book that you can easily progress from a reluctant speaker to a rising star to a pro. If you already consider yourself a good speaker,

---

[1] Franklin D. Roosevelt. (1933). First Inaugural Address of Franklin D. Roosevelt. *Current, February 2009* (510), 13-15.

with these tools and your added focus and dedication you will go from good to great and enjoy all the success that comes with it.

In truth, there is no single thing, no other personal quality that can add more value to your life than the ability to communicate effectively and to speak with confidence, conviction, and clarity. Look around you, whether it is at work, in your community, or at your congregation, those that truly stand out from the crowd, those that lead and set the pace do so with the use of their voices. Leadership and speaking abilities are two sides of the same coin.

Since practicing the very thing that you want to get better at is the key to improvement, the same is obviously true for speaking: the more you practice the better and more confident you'll get. Your value and prestige as an employee will increase, your professional opportunities will proliferate, and your circle of influence will expand exponentially.

In today's world, perhaps more than ever before, sound communication and presentation skills are highly sought after. It is a well-documented and well-supported fact that those who speak and communicate effectively are more likely more likely to earn higher incomes, have better careers, and often get improved opportunities[2]. Are you missing out on this potential?

I believe that with focus, dedication and persistence, we can learn almost anything - what one man or woman can do, any man or woman can do. It really just comes down to personal desire and your level of commitment – so how badly do you want it?

Some would try to convince us that when it comes to public speaking and communication, those that have a naturally extroverted predisposition have all the advantage over the introverts of the world. That may hold some small measure of

---

[2] Martin Zwilling. (2012, November 23). Every Entrepreneur Needs to Master Public Speaking. *Forbes,* 1-3.

truth, but I am convinced from personal experience that absolutely anyone can learn the art of public speaking.

Years ago, I was interviewed by *Canadian Business*[3], I was asked about how I was able to conquer my fear of public speaking, moving from a perceived introvert to an extrovert, from being fearful to fearsome on the platform. I spoke about my personal strategy where I created a self-feeding loop that incorporates continuous feedback into continuous perfecting. Research demonstrates the quintessential importance of public speaking in both the marketplace and within a broader social context; those who speak with cool confidence are seen by others as natural leaders and more intelligent people. Good communicators are even perceived as being more attractive[4]. So the question is: Do you want to be seen as a smart, confident, good looking leader?

This book won't actually make you better looking nor can I assert that it will make you smarter; after all there is only so much that one book can do. What I can wholeheartedly promise you is this: if you apply yourself and apply the speaking tips, tools and techniques held within the pages of this book you will have all you'll ever need to take charge of the lectern or podium and speak your truth with power, poise, and personal confidence.

---

[3] Adam McDowell. (2012, December 10). Why the world needs more introverts. *Canadian Business*, 1-6.

[4] Maddux, J. and Rogers, R. (1980). Effects of Source Expertness, Physical Attractiveness, and Supporting Arguments on Persuasion: A Case of Brains Over Beauty. *Journal of Personality and Social Psychology, 39*(2), 235-244.

SPEAK LIKE A PRO

Part 1

Content

There are always three speeches, for every one you actually give. The one you practiced, the one you gave, and the one you wish you gave - Dale Carnegie

Black on White

Speaking, like so many things in life, can actually be a great opportunity if you are willing to seize it. It can be an opportunity for you, the speaker, to communicate your thoughts and ideas to a waiting, and hopefully enthusiastic, audience. This opportunity, like so many others that life provides, is no small thing. For, whatever the duration or topic of your speech, you hold in your grasp the eyes and ears of your audience; by their presence you have been granted the gift of their valued time and attention. We are all given this tremendous opportunity and privilege of sharing something of ourselves and our ideas about what is important to us and hopefully meaningful to our audiences. It is an opportunity to impart new knowledge, to entertain, to inspire and to motivate. Above all else, it is an opportunity to communicate your heart and mind.

So seize that opportunity by making sure that you always honour them and their time with well-considered content that has been thoughtfully assembled and delivered with plenty of zing. Always strive to give them the very best delivery of your well-crafted and rehearsed speech. They deserve no less, nor should the speaker, ever deliver less. Never forget, that addressing any audience, no matter what size, age, gender or social grouping is an honour, a privilege and an opportunity to be seized.

Regardless of the kind of speech you have been asked to deliver, be it as the best man or bride's maid, a eulogy for the departed, a commencement address to inspire a new generation, a presentation at work, a workshop or an election speech to your condo board, this book is designed to help you get the job done.

When that eventful speaking date arrives, maybe it's even upon you right now, where you have the audience's attention in the grasp of your hands, what are you going to say? How are you going to say it so that you create an impact?

The language, structure, and delivery of a speech are all determined by the fact that it is, after all, a speech. A speech is different from a written work that has been designed to be read; a speech is meant to be heard. In short a good speech should feel and sound conversational in its tone.

This distinction may seem trivial at first, but believe me it makes all difference between a boring lecture (something simply read) and a dynamic presentation (something that is heard and felt). Understanding the difference between the two is tremendously important to your speaking success and your audience's interest.

Any speech, broken right down, can be reduced to a long series of spoken words; strung together into sentences and paragraphs. Words have specific sounds, meaning and relevance. Words with all their weight and history, reference and allusions are the building blocks that create truly memorable experiences for your audiences to enjoy.

Excellence in language is all about choosing your words and sentences carefully, paying particular attention to how they sound together and the meaning they denote. It is ultimately how you craft a spellbinding speech. One that is not only pleasing and engaging to listen to, but more importantly, one that is clear of purpose and meaningful to the hearts and minds of the audience.

A towering giant of purpose and meaning was Sir Winston Churchill; a political Titan to be sure and one of the greatest orators of the twentieth century. Churchill has left an indelible and incomparable legacy to the art of public speaking. Not only did he prepare and deliver so many great and immortalized speeches, coined many lasting and resonating phrases - both pithy and profound - he also expressed a keen interest in the subject and provided layers of perspective on the art of preparing and presenting good speeches.

For Churchill, colourful and expressive language was paramount. He spoke passionately on the astute usage of what he referred to as "CREAM" in the creation of impactful speeches - **C**ontrast, **R**hyme, **E**cho, **A**lliteration, and **M**etaphor[5]. Making ample use of this formula himself, Churchill repeatedly emphasized how these simple literary devices were absolutely indispensable to the successful creation of a fine personal speaking style and creating satisfying and memorable speeches. Using the above formula, we all have the opportunity to create words worth remembering and repeating.

Don't be afraid to dazzle your audiences with beautiful and expressive language that adds colour to your content. Deliver your messages and communicate your ideas with a bit of panache. The

---

[5] Humes, James. (2007). The Wit & Wisdom of Winston Churchill. New York: NY: Harper Collins.

following are examples of the inspired use of CREAM elements in action. You may recognize some. They all originated in famous speeches.

- "Ask not what your country can do for you; ask what you can do for your country." JFK[6]
  (Contrast, alliteration and echo)

- "A nation that forgets its past has no future." Churchill[7]
  (Metaphor, alliteration, and contrast)

- "Where there is a great deal of free speech, there is always a certain amount of foolish speech." Churchill[8]
  (Echo and contrast)

- "Not everything that can be counted counts and not everything that counts can be counted." Einstein[9]
  (Echo, alliteration, rhyme, and contrast)

- "In the End, we will remember not the words of our enemies, but the silence of our friends." Martin Luther King Jr.[10]
  (Contrast, alliteration, and echo)

---

[6] Kennedy, J. F. (1961). Inaugural Address. *The American Presidency Project*. Retrieved from http://www.presidency.ucsb.edu/ws/?pid=8032.

[7] Humes, James. (2007). The Wit & Wisdom of Winston Churchill. New York: NY: Harper Collins.

[8] Gilbert, M. (2005). Churchill and America. New York: NY: Free Press.

[9] Toye, F. (2015). "Not everything that can be counted counts and not everything that counts can be counted" (attributed to Albert Einstein). *British Journal of Pain, 9*(1), 7.

[10] "Martin Luther King, Jr. (1967). The Trumpet of Conscience. Boston: MA: Beacon Press.

As you can see from the above examples, words that have been carefully sculpted and patiently arranged into beautiful and poignant sentences have a deeper and longer lasting resonance. They create a deeper connection, and, as such, they are remembered long after they were first spoken.

It pays to remember that a speech is meant to be heard, not read. So think about how the words you have chosen sound together. Are they pleasing to hear together? Is there some pleasing internal rhythm or rhyme in the phrase? If not, then ask yourself how you can add some in some way? Always try to use vivid colours to paint your mental pictures and they will be much more compelling and convincing when heard.

That being said, one must always keep in mind that as with so many things less is often more. So resist the urge and don't overdo it. Your primary speaking purpose must be accomplished, that is your goal. Whether informing, entertaining, persuading, inspiring, or motivating, you must stay true to your purpose. The careful and astute selection of words and language is ultimately the means to your end, not the end in itself; expounding your core message or premise. Make sure the language you have selected clearly reflects what you want to say.

The Blinking Cursor

"The secret of getting ahead is getting started. The secret of getting started is breaking your complex overwhelming tasks into small manageable tasks, and then starting on the first one." — Mark Twain

Have you ever been at a loss for words when you needed them the most? At times my family wishes this would happen more often in my case. But if you have, you are not alone; my family's wish aside. I too have had my struggles whether in the writing of this book, a blog or a speech.

It is all too common to have faced that dreaded blank piece of paper or the incessant flicker of a cursor on the computer screen. It can be a daunting and even a debilitating thing to experience. The ugly beast of self-doubt can be crippling if you allow it in. If we make the mistake of allowing self-doubt in, the rising anxiety of self-imposed pressure to produce something can cause complete mental paralysis. With so many things to consider, and an almost infinite amount of variables to think about, how does one begin to write a speech? What comes first? Where should you start?

For many would be speakers, that bare white page or the blinking of the cursor on a computer screen can become a trap. What is often referred to as "writers block" can set in and cripple your efforts before you even get a chance to get started.

It doesn't have to be that way. Realize that you're putting way too much pressure on yourself. No one needs that kind of self-imposed pressure; right?

If you are having trouble getting started, simply step away from the page, go for a walk, do something else, and clear your mind. Remember that stress will pass, as it always does, and that everything will be okay. You've got to have faith. Keep in mind that no one ever starts with a final product. Any final product first requires an idea, brainstorming, planning, and prototypes; only then does the final product begin to emerge.

Start off with a broad open perspective or premise and then take small progressive steps in filling it out. Don't let yourself get overwhelmed by the demon of self-imposed pressure. Start by drawing out broad general ideas. Those ideas can then be nurtured so that they grow and become bigger, bolder and more elaborate. However, at first you'll want to keep things simple so that you can focus on your basic theme or message.

I prefer to start my speeches with a freshly pointed pencil and a simple pad of lined paper. At the top of the page I write down my very general theme or premise – for example "team-building" - then I try to generate lots of simple ideas related to my chosen topic. Asking and answering questions such as: What experiences have I had about "team building"? What have I read about it in books, magazines, or in the papers? What is my point of view? What is this like? Is there something new happening in this field?

First, I ask these and many other questions, only then do I start to flesh them out by building chunks of information, finding appropriate stories, anecdotes and analogies, eventually focusing everything into a core message. That message will ultimately be supported by my main points drawn from my research and the questions that I've asked.

Start with big broad ideas and concepts, and then focus in and flesh them out; all the while creating the supporting material that will validate your point of view. All that stuff that you will have compiled through your research.

If you are still stuck, confounded, or having trouble figuring out where to start, don't panic. There are a few trusted tools that will help you overcome the potential pitfall of writer's block and will keep your mind focused on the task at hand. Figuring out what you want to say and how you're going to say it. The process of building the core message and content we want to communicate to our audience simply starts by asking ourselves some important and pertinent questions.

If you have been asked or invited to speak at an event, you will need to consult and coordinate with the organizers. They may have something specific in mind that they would like you to speak about or a particular point they want covered. Obviously, in a case such as this, that is precisely where you would start. However, regardless of whether they have given you a specific topic or have a certain expectation, you should always ask your contact some simple questions in order to gain clarity, a deeper understanding of their expectations, and to elucidate and solidify the specifics concerning the event's logistics.

In the following chapter you will be introduced to the classic and essential W5 questions – those important things to ask yourself as you get started. Answering these questions is the first giant step towards creating the content that will connect and communicate, that is appropriate to whom your expected audience will be, and one that will be in-line with the tone or theme of the event.

Next, we will explore a few literary devices in some more detail. These devices will polish your content and make it shine like sunshine on a cloudy day making your content more attractive so that it can connect more deeply and be more impactful to your audience; because the key point to always remember is that you are always delivering a message to someone. You are playing the part of the messenger. Everything that you will ever say or do on the speaking platform must be entirely about and focused on benefiting your audience. Without them there is no purpose to your speech.

Before You Get Started

"If you have a dream, you can spend a lifetime studying, planning, and getting ready for it. What you should be doing is getting started" - Drew Houston

The content of a speech or presentation will always depend on determining crucial variables that come from simply answering these five basic time-honoured questions: who, what, where, when and why. Answering these questions provides you with a strong foundation for building your content in a meaningful and more focused way that will connect the right information. This crucial step should never be skipped. In order to achieve success you must set yourself up for success, by laying down the strong foundations that are imperative to your speaking success – do this every single time you speak. These questions appear to be relatively simple, however they should never be overlooked or taken for granted. Simplicity is so often the clearest path forward.

Knowing what to say is quintessential to assuring that you create the most appropriate presentation possible for a specific audience. The questions are unambiguously designed to help you create a strong structure that will successfully support your theme or message. They will help you decide on the most appropriate method of delivery to ensure a strong and clear communication of ideas allowing for a deeper connection to your audience.

Let's take a look at the W5 Questions:

- **Who is the audience?**
- **What do they need to hear?**
- **Where are you speaking?**
- **Why are you speaking?**
- **When are you speaking?**

Who is your intended audience?

This question may seem fairly obvious, however this question is paramount because everything we say during a speech must be focused on the specific audience we are addressing.

Audiences can vary significantly. Consider what you would say if you were speaking to adults as opposed to kids; professionals versus laypeople; at a wedding versus a funeral; or at a social versus a corporate event. Your content and message would depend on whom your intended audience might happen to be. Understand that what will be of interest to teenagers will rarely be the same as what interests senior executives at a business meeting or the guests at a loved one's wedding. Knowing your audience is essential to crafting a meaningful message and content that connects.

Absolutely everything contained within your speech is dependent on determining this with as much precision as possible. Talk to the organizers and/or your contact for the event for more information on the actual audience make-up.

Years ago, when I first began speaking professionally, I was once asked to deliver an inspirational keynote address, thanking a group of volunteers for their hard work and dedication over the course of a fund-raising campaign. I prepared what I thought would be a truly inspirational speech for the audience. I dressed in my best suit and arrived at the event with my prepared speech, convinced that I would connect strongly with this altruistic adult audience. However, when I arrived at the venue, I quickly and rather embarrassingly realized that the volunteers were all young adults and teenagers: there was virtually no one over the age of twenty-one.

Needless to say, I was overdressed and probably looked pretty stuffy. I quickly grasped that my intended message wouldn't connect to the audience gathered in the hall in the way that I had planned. I knew that my message had a universal appeal but the content of my stories, anecdotes, and metaphors didn't reflect this particular audience. They would have a hard time relating to my content. I had committed the deadly sin of assuming too much. In retrospect, the fact that the venue was scheduled to take place in a local high school should have set off some alarm bells and so I was the like a deer caught in the headlights due to my assumption.

I quickly and somewhat clumsily modified the content of my speech on the back of a napkin minutes before taking the platform. I lost the jacket and tie, unbutton my shirt collar, rolled up my sleeves, and simplified the language of my original message into something more casual. I punched in a few more appropriate stories and delivered the speech in a more humorous way. And yes, I included some teenage jargon, which probably made me look a little lame but hopefully endearing too, and I topped it off by namedropping a few celebrities. It was clumsy but I did my best and got through it.

What on earth did we ever do before smartphones and instant access to the web? That day I truly realized the power of technology; smartphones, google and the internet. I learned an important lesson that day, never assume anything, always check all the facts, and most importantly; know your audience.

Take a moment to reflect on your own experiences as an audience member or participant at a lecture, workshop or presentation. Have you ever felt that the content was inappropriate for the audience in question? Maybe the information was too abstract, perhaps too general, or maybe lacked cultural diversity in the stories and examples that were used. Perhaps the speaker foolishly made some assumptions about who the audience was.

There are many different types of speeches, workshops, and presentations and you have probably been an audience member for one or more of them. Whether it was workplace training, a commencement address, a religious sermon, or a motivational speech given by your favorite personal development guru, did the speaker connect to you specifically? How did you feel as an audience member? Why and how did they connect to you as an audience member? If you did feel a connection with the speaker and his or her content, it was likely because the speaker had prepared and understood their specific audience; who they were, what made them tick, and what they wanted or needed to hear. Making sure that we match the audience to the right type of presentation is absolutely crucial for effective and clear communication to take place. For example, a eulogy at a funeral might not be the most appropriate time to deliver a humorous speech or explore a racy or raunchy subject. Likewise an after dinner talk will probably not provide you with the right audience for a somber subject or something too intellectually demanding. Getting this right is an important aspect to creating content and to your speaking success.

Will the audience be formal or casual? Do they share a common profession? Will they be young or more seasoned? Will they be mostly men or mostly women? Will they be ethnically diverse? These and many other considerations should be explored as you begin to prepare the "right" content of your speech or presentation. In essence, you must consider what the audience needs to know.

Right Language, Right Audience

Another important consideration, one that we have already touched upon, is your selection of words and your use of language. For instance, the complexity of your concepts or whether to use industry jargon will likewise depend on the makeup of your audience. Professionals at an association meeting or industry conference will expect a certain amount of technocratic jargon. However if you try to use this same type to technocratic language with an audience of lay-people, you will quickly lose their interest, you may even cause them to resent you, and you will simply not get your message through to them at all, and you will have failed in your purpose.

A sound rule of thumb is to always use simple and easily understood words and to likewise keep your sentences short and simple in structure. Make it as easy as possible for your audiences to understand you. Remember that you must communicate to all, and that means both the least and most knowledgeable members of the group. Never allow yourself to only speak to the cleverest few in the audience. It may seem counter-intuitive but you must always break it down to make sure that everyone gets it. If you want to prove that you're clever, join a local Mensa group[11].

Clear communication is the name of the game so keep your language simple. The human brain, like a computer, can only process a certain amount of information at any given time, so simple clear language is more readily understood. If every word has to be decoded, audiences will likely miss some of the information that is being presented. Keep it simple.

Another key consideration is whether your audience is composed of non-native speakers. When addressing such an audience you will want to speak both slowly and clearly, using simple short sentences and avoiding too many esoteric cultural references, jargon, or buzzwords as much as possible.

Knowing and being aware of your audience makeup is crucial to the appropriate development of your content. As you can see, how we choose to say it largely depends on who we are saying it to.

So before you sit in front of that blank page or computer screen to write your speech or presentation in earnest, it is crucial that you speak to the event contact person to get all the pertinent details about the audience you will be delivering to. Ensure that they can get you the answers to the questions listed below. Your very first questions should be about whom will make up the audience:

- What is the audience makeup?
- How many people are expected to attend?
- What is the purpose of the speech? (to inform, entertain, motivate, persuade, inspire)
- How long are you expected to speak for?
- Will it be a formal or casual event?

---

[11] Mensa. (2017). *About Mensa International*. Retrieved from http://www.mensa.org

- What is the average age of the audience?
- Is it mostly men or women or both?
- Is English their first language?

This is just a sampling; there are many more questions that you could ask, so if an idea pops into your head, don't be afraid to ask. Before connecting with your contact, write out as many pertinent questions as you can think of. Don't be shy about it. Remember it is better to ask lots of questions early on in the process than it is to get unpleasant surprises when you finally arrive to present your prepared speech.

What do they need to hear?

Now that you have a better and more detailed understanding of who you will be speaking to the next and equally important W5 question to consider is what does the audience need to hear?

Here is where we dive deeply into what your content will be. What should be the theme or central message of your presentation or speech? Right away you can see how understanding audience makeup directly ties into the potential substance of your content and your approach to it. The content, your points, meaning and message, the level of detail and your point of view, are all determined by the type of speech or presentation that you will be delivering, how much time you have, and of course the audience makeup.

Every single audience that you will ever address is exactly the same in one very significant aspect: they are all tuned to the same Radio station **WIIFM,** or **what's in it for me?** Every member of every audience, whether conscious of it or not, will always be asking that key central question; what's in it for me? In fact, I am certain that you have asked yourself this very question, every single time you have been an audience member yourself.

Therefore, your presentation must be "YOU" (the audience) focused. In other words, it must be entirely focused on your audience's needs and wants. The role of a speaker is to inform, motivate, inspire, persuade or entertain. Whether this happens successfully or not is almost entirely dependent on the questions you ask and the choices you make.

Let's have a look at some of the different types of speeches and presentations that are out there.

- **The Keynote Address** – ranging from 30 to 90 minutes in duration. A Keynote is a high level, high concept thematic speech. Often it is the main attraction of a conference or convention and the first or last presentation of the event. It is usually motivational or inspirational in tone, with a powerful take away message or a strong call to action.

- **Speeches** – Ranging anywhere from just a minute to thirty minutes or more in duration. Speeches can be humorous, entertaining, motivational, persuasive, inspirational or informative. Included in this category are wedding speeches, boardroom or business speeches, commencement addresses, eulogies, and acceptance speeches. There are many other occasions that call for speeches and an exhaustive list is almost impossible to compile. In short, a speech is a thematically structured talk presented in front of an audience consisting of an opening, a body and a conclusion.

- **Workshop/Seminar/Plenary Session** – These largely interchangeable types of presentations are usually informative in nature and can vary in duration from an hour to multiple day training events. These facilitated presentations are usually highly interactive, where participants are all working together or in sub-groups towards a common learning objective. Essentially these are adult learning sessions, often taking place in a quasi-classroom format.

The type of speech or presentation you choose will help set the scene for the selection, arrangement, and presentation of your content. As you can see from the above list, there are substantial differences in the required preparation and approach. You might need to research some facts and figures to support your statements and conclusions; relevant stories to help illuminate; perhaps you'll need to find, develop, and tickle your funny bone for more engagement; maybe you want to reminisce through poignant stories, or you may want to combine some portion of them all. This is entirely up to you and the research you have done, your audience, and the type of speech or presentation that you will be delivering. However you should always remember to make sure that you are broadcasting loud and clear on everyone's favorite radio station - WIIFM.

- I have included outlines for a variety of speeches in an Appendix at the back of this book. Simply select the type of speech that you need to prepare and the guide will help you develop and structure your content. They have been specifically designed to help you get started by providing you with the basic "must haves" and "must dos" for the given speech. If you follow the instructions and advice, they are virtually foolproof.

Where are you speaking?

The next W5 question is relatively simple and straightforward one to answer, but as we have learned, never assume. It is worthwhile to make sure that you have clarified any assumptions and understand where will you be speaking?

This question, like the others we have reviewed together, is also an important one to consider for several reasons. You need to communicate clearly with the organizers and make sure that every logistical consideration has been addressed regarding both the location of the event and from where you will be speaking. It is not merely a question of location, as important as that obviously is, where you will present has many other implications that must be ironed out. Again, never ever assume anything, always get the facts straight.

- Is travel involved? If so, what are the arrangements and who covers the cost? Be clear and get it in writing.

- How will you get there – by limousine (wouldn't that be nice), transit or taxi, or with your own vehicle; if so, where do you park specifically? How long will the trip take in traffic? Will you need special access to the building or venue?

- Where will you be speaking? Is there an elevated platform or stage? Will there be a lectern or podium provided? What room or hall? Get exact directions. Will someone be meeting you? Get their cell phone number.

- Is a microphone provided or must you speak without one? If yes, what kind? (lapel, hand held, cordless) Will there be a sound check beforehand that you will be required to attend?

- What about technical logistics such as the use of overhead projection and handouts? Will there be a computer, projector and screen available for your use? How do you get you files to them - USB thumb drive? - and finally, who will distribute handouts and how many will you need to print and bring?

I always make every effort to visit the venue before I speak and so I always arrive early in order to get a feel for the space beforehand. I walk the stage and get comfortable with the speaking area and its size. Arriving early also gives you ample opportunity to fine tune logistical concerns such as where can you wait while you are being introduced and how you will get on and off the stage.

Often there are minor and unanticipated issues that you will need to deal with, so make sure you give yourself lots of spare time for the unexpected. There have been times where I have arrived at a venue expecting a projector and screen to be set up, only to end up running around because it was overlooked. Getting there early can be a life saver.

There are more benefits to arriving early. It provides a great opportunity to network with key players and to deepen your connection to the organizers and the event. In terms of content, you can also "work the room" creating a rapport with the audience even before you speak and "mine" them for tidbits of information, water cooler stories, successes, problems or funny tidbits that you can easily weave into your speech. Incorporating those little tidbits will make your content even more relevant, timely, and appropriate. Doing this can have a huge impact on the audience, they love it when you make some insider reference tailor made for the audience and it's often a great way to get a few laughs and create better rapport.

Depending on the event, venue, or type of speech, little or none of the above might be relevant, however always make sure that you know where you will be speaking and verify that all the logistics associated with the location have been arranged beforehand. Nevertheless, no matter what, always try to arrive early.

Why are you speaking?

AN interesting question for you to consider now is why are you speaking to this particular audience? What is your personal or professional motivation for speaking to them? Why them, why you, and why this subject matter in particular? Understanding this is a profoundly important element of creating content.

To me "why" is the most profound of all the questions that we could possibly ask and the answers to "why" are often the most interesting and enlightening. The question always leads us to first causes, internal motivations, our core values, and other pertinent information. "Why" is the question that is at the heart of our boundless human curiosity. It led our ancestors out of their caves to spread out across the entire world and it is the cornerstone of every invention we have happened upon. "Why" has an immensely profound power.

So ask yourself why you are speaking to this particular audience? What gifts or skills do you possess that you are willing and able to share with this group? Why are they relevant to this audience? Why should they listen to you? A good speaker can easily answer these questions with just a mere thought upon the subject, however a truly great speaker has completely internalized his or her reasons and internal motivations; their "why" affects and informs their entire approach to speaking and it is the nucleus of their modus operandi.

Asking and answering the question "why" is so much more than an esoteric or existential question to ponder philosophically. Although I do encourage you to think deeply about why you want to speak, it is a means to discovering and understanding your passion and the gifts you have to offer. This is a way of getting personal clarity about your purpose.

What are the unique and relevant talents and skills that you have to offer; your experiences, stories, sense of humour, information, insights and knowledge you have acquired through your life? What knowledge do you have that your audiences can benefit from?

In large part, the answer to the question of "why you are speaking?" will end up being summarized, stylized and itemized as the details of your introduction. The audience wants to know who you are and why you are speaking to them. Are you a Subject Matter Expert (SME) or a specialist of some kind? Have you had an experience that gave you special insight into something we all hold in common? The audience needs some context in order for them to grant you their acceptance.

Whatever your reasons might be for speaking, you must align these two concepts; why are you speaking to this audience and what's in it for them? Getting a handle as to why you are speaking gives you the necessary tools that are essential to creating a much deeper connection with your audience. Once you know and understand where you are coming from and what you have to offer so the audience can clearly understand what's in it for them.

For me, the answer to the question "why" is simple. I find personal fulfilment when I am able to help others help themselves. I believe in the boundless potential of every living soul and that I have the ability to shine a light to show them the way. By sharing my unique experiences, insights, and the knowledge I have acquired over the course of my life; I have the privilege of helping my audiences help themselves. Take the time right now to answer your "why".

When are you speaking?

A couple of years ago I was invited to speak to a group of business people in Toronto's Financial District at "7:30". It was to be an hour long workshop and they marketed it widely and had anticipated full audience attendance. Essentially I was the only item on the agenda for that meeting. At 7:45 in the morning I received a call on my cell phone. It was the organizer for my 7:30 event that day. He was frantic and almost out of breath as he kept asking me where I was "right now"? Puzzled by his exasperation, I told him where I was and asked him if everything was okay. He said, "Are you almost here? The room is full and everyone is wondering where you are". "Why would they be there, I'm not speaking for another twelve hours", I replied. Then I finally got it, understood what had happened, and why he was frantic.

I had assumed that the event was taking place at 7:30 pm. Wrong! It was happening right now. Unfortunately, there was no possible way on earth that I could have gotten to that event in a reasonable amount of time. In fact, if I had left right away, I would have made it there in time to greet the audience as they left. My assumption about "when" I was expected to speak had created a very embarrassing situation for me and more importantly for the organizers of the event. Needless to say, it tarnished my reputation, and consequently, I have never been invited back to speak to that group. I can't blame them for feeling that way – *mea culpa*.

It arose from a silly and almost trivial misunderstanding. More than just a few emails had been sent back and forth between myself and the organizers, yet at no point in time was there any specification whether 7:30 was to be morning or evening – I never asked and they never said – we both assumed. Because I most often speak in the afternoon or evening, I had simply assumed that I was scheduled for 7:30 in the evening. They assumed that I knew it was a morning event. Getting the "when" clearly answered is crucial.

If you are one of several booked speakers on a particular day, and of course when you yourself will be speaking, you should always find out how many other speakers will be speaking before, and how many will be speaking once you are done,. Numerous things can go wrong, there are last minute changes to the agenda or even last-minute speaker cancellations, sometimes a speaker goes too long or too short and everything on the agenda must be re-tweaked in order to stick to the timeline and make it all work.

I was once at a conference where the fire alarm went off in the middle of a presentation and everyone was forced to evacuate. Thankfully, I wasn't the presenter. However all the other speakers on the agenda had to shift their speaking time, shorten their prepared speeches on the fly. One speaker had to be dropped from the agenda entirely. The point is that you never can tell what might happen, so know when you are speaking and be prepared for the unexpected.

Another brilliant advantage to arriving early is that when there are multiple speakers booked, you have an opportunity to find out as much information and as many details as possible concerning the various topics that will be covered. These are important opportunities because it affords you the opportunity to avoid repeating a quote, a joke or finding out if part of your message has already been delivered by another speaker. You can tweak your content accordingly. Incorporating some points from other speakers as "call-backs" is the mark of a professional thinking on his or her feet.

Arriving early gives you the time to review your speech, incorporate "call-backs", and shorten or stretch your presentation as the need arises. If you want to shine like a star, incorporate part of what another speaker has said into your speech as a call-back. Audiences love this stuff and it makes you look confident. I recommend that you get as much information about any other speaker and their content when you first speak to your contact or organizer. In fact you may want to contact the other speaker(s) to talk to them about what they plan to cover.

Here are some questions to consider:

- How many other speakers are on the agenda?
- What are their topics, themes, or messages?
- When in the program agenda are you slotted to speak?
- Get there early and be ready for the unexpected.
- Get all the specific details and times in writing.

Are you speaking first thing in the morning to a sleepy group, perhaps you are speaking just before or after lunch where the audience is either hungry or a little lethargic after eating? These considerations matter when building content and should be incorporated into your preparations.

The content you choose must be considered and be appropriate to the time slot. Are you the first speaker? Setting the theme and tone for the entire conference or are you the last speaker of the event, recapping the theme, summing things up, and giving the audience a motivational take away message; a call to action. All these factors must be considered when developing and shaping the content of your speech or presentation. Again, know exactly when you are speaking and then arrive early and get familiar with the stage, the equipment, and all the logistics.

Now that we have gotten started by looking at the W5 questions in some detail, let's get started on designing and building the content of the speech or presentation. In the next section we will uncover some easy steps for creating great content that connects.

Let's Get Started...

The Message

"Whatever words we utter should be chosen with care for people will hear them and be influenced by them for good or ill" - Buddha

We all have things and ideas that we believe in and care deeply about, we all have points of view and perspectives. We have thoughts about how we think things should be and in a word we all have passions. In translating those ideas into key messages that are focused on an audience and their sense of WIIFM, we have, in essence, the raw material to create the foundation for our speeches, presentations and workshops.

It's all about the message! When it comes to the central message of your speech, it must be absolutely crystal clear; which is why we spent time exploring and answering our W5 questions earlier. Lackluster speeches often fail because the speaker was unsure or unclear about his or her own message. Think about it, if you cannot clearly and succinctly articulate your own message or theme in a few concise and well-chosen words then you cannot expect your audience members to understand your message either. If you are confused or unclear about your message, you can bet that your audience will be just as confused and unclear about your message.

When I work with speakers in the development and perfection of their presentations, I always ask them to give me a synopsis. "Paint me a picture explaining the core message - the central theme – that thing that you want the audience to get out of your talk; state it as briefly as possible, tell me what's it all about?" Sadly, the stumbled and stammered response that I get is, at best, a fuzzy and unclear picture. After they have said 50-75 words, I simply cut them off. They typically protest, "But I was just about to get to my point". It shouldn't ever require a speech to present a synopsis of a speech. At that point it's clear that they still haven't isolated the gist of the message. They simply need to ask more questions and spend some more time thinking about their message.

It is practically impossible to write an effective speech that communicates a clear point of view, if you're unable to articulate your message succinctly and with absolute clarity. You've got to get it down to one short sentence. That solid foundation, properly set, will support the structure, content, and the eventual delivery of your speech with all the pizzazz and panache it deserves. Consider the following questions:

- What is the central theme that you want to convey?
- Is your message focused on one idea?
- Is it clear and understandable? *I suggest that you ask a family member, friend or colleague if they understand your message.*

Reflect on some of what have been considered the greatest and most memorable speeches from our recent history. Dr. Martin Luther King Jr's *I Have a Dream*, JFK's *Inaugural Address*, or Churchill's, *We shall never yield*. I'm sure that you are at least somewhat familiar with them, however, if you have never heard or read them in their entirety, then I strongly encourage you to do so right now. They are all easily accessible through an internet search. These brilliantly crafted speeches have been immortalized and etched on our collective memories precisely because of the complete clarity of their messages. The words resonate and echo decades later and they have been quoted more times than you could shake a stick at.

Cut the Crap

Once you have your clearly focused message ready, it will become the very foundation of your entire speech or presentation and everything that you say must be tied to it, support it, and relate to it. As you flesh out the content of your speech, if some part of your content doesn't support your message, get rid of it right away – in short, cut the crap. I repeat, if any content does not support your core message, you must get rid of it right away before you start getting too attached to it. I have more than once held onto content that did not support my message because I thought it was clever, or that it was such a well-crafted sentence. The longer I held onto it the harder it became to let it go. Clarity is King, so if it doesn't help, it will most likely hinder clear communication.

As you add stories, humour and your various other points, you must be constantly asking yourself, "How does this relate to or support my central message?" and then have courage and be absolutely ruthless in your commitment to your message. Again, everything, yes absolutely and unequivocally everything that you add to your speech must relate back to and support your central message – no exceptions, ever. As Zig Ziglar has said, "don't be a wandering generality, rather be a meaningful specific"[12].

If, while you are speaking in front of an audience, you allow yourself to go all over the map, taking off on unrelated tangents, constantly adding irrelevant little asides, you will invariably lose some, if not all of your audience members as they struggle to understand the point you are trying to make. The audience needs to understand the interconnectivity and relevance of what you are saying. It should never be a struggle for the audience to follow your train of thought. They haven't come for wandering generalities but rather they have come for meaningful specifics imparted to them through the clarity of your message. Your job is to make it as easy as possible for them to understand and relate to what you are saying.

---

[12] Ziglar.com. (2017). *Meaningful Specific*. Retrieved from https://www.ziglar.com/quotes/meaningful-specific/

A long time ago, while attending University, I once had a professor that was notorious for the fact the he never ever seemed to make a point. Not a great quality in a professor. He would seemingly start off his lectures with the best of intentions, but, perhaps because he wanted us to be spellbound by his immense knowledge - which he undoubtedly had – he never quite seemed to ever make his point – that is if he had one to make. He was a very clever man yet unable to convey his intended message because he couldn't or wouldn't stick to the central message of his lecture. We students suffered as a consequence. Thankfully he has since retired. Don't let your audiences suffer the absence of clarity.

Remember everyone is always tuned to WIIFM. As we discussed earlier, the human brain can only actively process a limited amount of information at any given time, clarity and sound structure are paramount to the brain's processing power, so keep them interested by keeping your core message simple and completely focused.

I was getting a one-on-one coaching session by the extraordinary professional speaker Mark Hunter a few years ago. He was at that time the reigning World Champion of Public Speaking. We were working together on one of my speeches, a speech that I had just written and one that I felt pretty good about – it had real potential, or so I thought. On the first reading, he tore it to pieces. Mark is a kind and gentle man and so he did so in the gentlest and kindest way possible. In doing so he showed me how I actually had three separate, and at times, conflicting messages all within the span of a ten minute speech. He taught me that by asking a series of well thought out questions, just as we have done above, that there was a real need of clarity in my speech. I had had a sense of it but you see, in the writing of the speech, I had become really attached to certain sentences and the way the words sounded together and the images that they painted. I was confounding the core message that I wanted to covey by refusing to let those pet phrases and pretty words go. They sounded good but added nothing to the message. In fact they had become separate messages that were confusing my intended core message.

No wonder I was having trouble connecting to my audience with that speech. After cutting, editing and reworking that speech and refocusing on a clear singular core message, it became a brilliant, funny, and poignant speech. More importantly, my audiences could now effortlessly connect to my message. It was a tough and humbling lesson to learn but one that I have never forgotten.

So ask yourself, "What is your message?" If you have trouble articulating it, ask lots of questions, then using the answers, narrow it down until you can articulate it in one or two short sentences.

Stories

"You're never going to kill storytelling, because it's built into the human plan. We come with it" - Margaret Atwood

Stories are how we describe ourselves, our experiences and the world in which we live. On any typical Monday morning when your coworkers ask you to recount what you did on the weekend you invariably answer through the telling of a story. If you really think about it, more than anything else, when we speak to others, we tend to tell stories. Consequently, the most important ingredient of any speech or presentation that you deliver will be the stories that you choose to tell to support your points. After all, as the old saying goes, "everyone loves a good story". Yet it is shocking how often speakers completely omit stories from their presentations.

When my kids were younger, they couldn't fall asleep without my first reading them their favorite bedtime stories. It is a ritual as old as mankind that is equally true in every culture all around the world. Our forefathers entertained themselves in the evenings by sharing stories depicting the heroes of battle, sharing cautionary tales, or folktales and myths. For eons, much of our early human knowledge was passed from one generation to another through the vehicle of stories. They encapsulated all our knowledge, lessons, and cultural history. Even today, we love relating stories about our weekend adventures and escapades, and many revel in the recounting of salacious gossipy tales. In truth we are all personified stories with a beginning, a body, and an eventual end. Stories are the vehicles by which we drive our morals, our ethics, our philosophies, our truth, our humour and our lessons.

In a speech stories magically transform what might otherwise be dry and dull information into understandable, relatable, and memorable bits of information. Creating an emotional rapport that pierces through the heart, and then serendipitously opens the doors to the mind, stories create memorable connections and allow for clear communication – they provide a sense of curiosity, emotion, and drama.

Finally, so many of the great and important lessons of the past were captured in myths and tales permeated with stories – great philosophical truths told through the compelling power of stories that allowed the listener to connect to it emotionally. Once heard and internalized, we can easily remember and relate the messages we have heard like those of David and Goliath, Snow White, or the ancient Greek myths of Icarus or Sisyphus.

So make sure to incorporate lots of stories into your speeches or presentations and you'll see how the audience listens attentively and connects more deeply to your message.

Here are a few important points to remember when integrating stories into your speeches:

Personalize your story

The best stories are always personal stories. You are the best, and perhaps the only, authority when it comes to your own life experiences so no one can tell it like you can. Use your own personal stories to make you and your points more relatable to your audience. There are great lessons to be found in the seemingly trivial and mundane so don't feel like you have to be the hero of your own story.

Make sure you know what the message or point of your story is. If you aren't quite sure, relate it to a few people and ask them what message they feel the story conveys – you'll sometimes be surprised at what you get back. And remember that personal stories create a strong sense of credibility and rapport.

Set the scene
A story whether fictional or non-fictional, fantastical or historical, always happens at a certain time and place. Essentially when you set the scene you are answering two questions: where is this taking place? When is this taking place? It isn't necessary to describe every single detail of the scene or the time in which it occurs, however some situational detail is required to get the audience's imagination started in a certain time and place.

Create Conflict
All great stories are built around the resolution of some kind of conflict. That's after all where the drama lies. So make sure to create a sense of conflict early on in the story. A good rule of thumb is to introduce the conflict within the first third of the story. Conflict is what gets the audience emotionally invested by creating a sense of stress or anxiety that must subsequently be resolved. That feeling of satisfaction they get through the resolution of the conflict is the hook.

Use Characters
Characters are the essential component of any good story since the action happens through them. They make stories dramatic, dynamic and multi-dimensional. We relate to, empathise and

sympathise with, love or hate, and root for or revile the characters in stories – in short we get emotionally invested in them and what happens to them. Make sure that you describe your characters through a few well-chosen details. If you give too much description, you'll kill the audience's imagination, and it is though our imaginations that we are able to place ourselves within the story. Also, rather than just using a narrator's voice throughout the story, give your characters a voice my making them speak through dialogue. Here's a little secret: You'll often get the biggest laughs through well timed dialogue.

Bring it to a Climax
The conflict that you established early on in the story must come to its ultimate climax. How will the conflict resolve itself? It is the successful resolution of a conflict through a dramatic climax that allows us to use stories for the delivery of our meaning, message or moral. The climax is the threshold that must be traversed in order for the lesson to be learned and for transformation to occur. Think: What is the lesson that we should take away from the story?

Humour
I have heard it said many times that if you want to get paid as a speaker, you must make your audiences laugh. I couldn't agree more! Humour is imperative to a great presentation. It relieves some of the stress and tension that you have purposefully created and built up through the conflicts in your stories. Humour can also just simply be used to lighten the mood and provide a bit of light hearted entertainment. Whatever the type of presentation, you will seldom go wrong with the judicious use of well-timed humour.

An important point to note is that you should always strive to uncover the humour within your story. Never ever use canned jokes, especially jokes found on the internet; chances are that someone has already heard the joke. Canned jokes rarely fit the story and often come across feeling a bit forced - like squeezing a square peg into a round hole.

Find, or even better yet, reveal the humour within the story, within the setting, or amongst the characters. Exaggerate some aspect or detail of character to the verge of the ridiculous with a funny comparison. A tip to getting a good laugh is to place the joke in the mouth of a character through dialogue. It's an easy way of exploiting the funny side of miscommunication and misdirection.

Humour is an important key to connecting with your audience, whether you're lessening the tension in the room after saying something serious or just simply being entertaining, getting a smile and some laughter is priceless.

This list is by no means comprehensive. It is really just intended as a basic and generic outline to get you thinking about the components of stories and how to use them as integral elements in your speeches. There are countless books, CD's and other products on storytelling out there and I strongly urge you to pick some up and spend some time doing some of your own research on the subject. It will be an invaluable investment of your time that will surely pay off in dividends many times over.

The bottom line is that an effective speaker must be a good storyteller. There are no two ways about it. However it is wise to remember that the very best and most successful speakers are the ones that use storytelling by recounting their own personal stories, setting the scene, creating early conflict through the dialogue of their compelling characters, building their stories to a dramatic climax, and then always finishing them off by making strong and meaningful points followed by a call to action – all this while using liberal amounts of humour.

When recounting personal stories, it's common to want to paint ourselves in the best possible light by playing or portraying ourselves as a hero in our attempt to impress. Be careful to temper this tendency. No one likes a bragger. Even if you have climbed

Mount Everest, the most interesting parts of stories like that are the challenges you overcome, the unexpected failings, and the self-doubt that had to be conquered. The audience tends to be more interested in relating to your similarities than knowing that you are very special – even though I'm sure that you are.

So stay grounded and let your audiences know that you are human just like them. A very important point that I learned from the brilliant speaker Patricia Fripp is to not be afraid to share your failures, misunderstandings, and personal or professional shortcomings through your stories. These struggles and challenges humanize you as a speaker and will go a long way in making you more relatable by creating a sense of sympathy or empathy in the audience. After all, everyone has had to overcome some struggles through the course of their lives. Share your struggles with them and then share the life lessons that you gleaned as a result. Keep in mind that you only ever have to reveal what you are comfortable sharing. That being said you should always make sure that you remain positive in your messaging and in the points that you make as a result.

Using Facts and Figures

"If the facts don't fit the theory, change the facts" -Albert Einstein

The effective use and incorporation of facts, figures, and statistics can really bolster and add an awful lot of credibility to your speech. Supporting your points with facts and stats is oftentimes a necessary component of a good speech – especially in a boardroom or corporate setting - at other times facts and stats can help drive your message and provide the audience with powerful proof for your message.

Unfortunately, many of us have, at times, sat through boring lectures or PowerPoint presentations where the facts and figures acted more like sleeping pills that supporting points – given the choice of a boring lecture we'd often rather watch paint dry. The misuse of facts and figures can and must be avoided because, as obvious as it is, it's pretty important that your audience stays awake for the duration of your presentation. So don't ever let yourself be guilty of inducing sleep.

Your audience will frequently consist of a mixed bag of personalities, many of whom have a strong need and reliance on the objective support of facts and figures. They need them as validation to your message and to accept your credibility as an authority on the subject. If you are standing at the front of the room asserting a whole bunch of "truths" without citing or supporting them, your audience may have some trouble believing those "truths" – especially if they are hard to grasp or seem a little far-fetched, out of the ordinary or even unexpected. Sometimes, we need and want objective proof to give ourselves permission to believe a message or point that we are unsure of. No one ever wants to feel like they are being taken for a ride so a little support can go a long way when well used.

When the purpose of your presentation is to provide information, the ability to animate and relate your facts and figures in an interesting, agreeable, meaningful or playful way is crucial to a successfully engaging presentation. The ability to effortlessly and compellingly weave data into your speeches is a vital tool that you will need to have in spades. Getting this right will bring you to excellence in the art of speaking.

How can you take and transform the often dry and drab statistical material that supports your speech and make it sparkle with pizzazz and panache? The good news is that it's not as hard as you might think. It all comes down to how you say it and how you display it. Knowing the right amount of information to share is where you want to start. Always strive to use the least amount of data as possible. The idea is to provide just as much as is needed so that you have sufficiently supported your point. Numbers, graphs, and charts can be overwhelming for many therefore being judicious and striking the right balance is so important. You don't want to confound your audiences with unnecessary numbers and graphs – remember that less is more – when you push too much information on the audience, you end up pushing the audience out. Their minds will go numb and they'll simply tune out. Only use what is absolutely necessary to support and elaborate your points and conclusions and no more. Again, it's about clarity.

Once you have decided and determined the right amount of data that you need to support your point or conclusion, you will want to find a way to incorporate those facts and figures in a compelling and relatable way through the use of anecdotes, analogies or stories. A good story is a brilliant and highly effective way to transform dry and drab information into an easy to understand and relatable format while allowing for the emotional weight it needs and deserves.

For example, rather than presenting a bunch of stats or figures it is much more effective to recount a personal story incorporating all the relevant information right into the story itself. Tug at their heart strings and you'll gain access to their minds. Stories create an emotional hook, we see ourselves as the characters in the story, and we get emotionally invested in the action – especially if the story is both well-structured and well told - so using a good story as a vehicle to drive your information and make it relevant and memorable is a must-have technique and one that your audiences will love and appreciate.

Before I ever found and trained myself to speak in public, I was just like three out of every four people in the US – terrified of speaking in public[13]. Did you know that it's the number one fear; more that sharks, spiders, and even death? I wanted to get better so I spent

---

[13] Ingraham, C. (2014, October 30). America's top fears: Public speaking, heights and bugs. *The Washington Post*, 1-3.

$200 on books. That represents just a tiny drop in the $3 billion dollar a year self-help industry. Then I found Toastmasters. A ninety year old non-profit organization, with chapters in over a hundred counties with a quarter million members, it changed everything for me.

Again, it comes down to how you say it. Here's another example; rather than just simply stating a fact, interpret it in a meaningful way and add a little creativity in the mix for fun. So instead of just saying that 30% of people are considered to be unattractive, you could say "one in three" - it's much more direct and relatable. An even better and more creative way to present it would be to say: "Everybody please stand up. They say that one in three people are considered unattractive. Well, have a look to your left, now have a look to your right; if it's not one of them then it must be you". They'll burst into laughter but you'll have made a strong point. In this case, it's always easier to find the fault in others.

I live in Toronto where we have some very long commute times – on average over 60 minutes every day[14]. A more impactful way to convey the data would be to say, "Folks, on average, we spend so much time commuting that over the course of our working lives the average Torontonian will have spent over two full years of their lives simply getting to work and home again". That has impact.

Remember that your facts and figures must be presented in a way that creates impact with the audience otherwise those facts will not support your points or message. So try exploring new, interesting and creative ways to interpret and present your facts and figures. If you can present them emotionally, they will stick to the minds of your audiences.

---

[14] Statistics Canada. (2011). *Table 2: Usual commuting time to work, census metropolitan areas, 2011.* Retrieved from http://www12.statcan.gc.ca/nhs-enm/2011/as-sa/99-012-x/2011003/tbl/tbl02-eng.cfm

The Goldilocks median is what you want to find. Not too much and not too little is the right amount when it comes to using facts and figures. Too much information will confound your audiences and too little will leave them unconvinced, so use only what is needed to properly support your points. And once you have that amount figured out, weave them into stories or find other creative ways to connect the information with the audience emotionally.

In this section we have explored how to build relevant and relatable content for a specific type of speech or presentation to be delivered to a specific audience. In the following section we will look at how we can structure that content so that it more effectively communicates your message in an enjoyable, memorable and impactful way.

SPEAK LIKE A PRO

Part 2

Structure

"A talk is a voyage with purpose and it must be charted. The man, who starts out going nowhere, generally gets there." — Dale Carnegie

In the previous section, we asked and answered questions designed to create content. We've thought about our core message – and that everything we say in our speech must relate back to it - and the importance of great stories that illustrate the points we're making. In effect, we thought about and built our content. We have our material. Now we need to put it all together into a final product. We need to structure our content. Structure is the vehicle that drives our content home. When used effectively, structure organizes your content so that it can be easily and effectively communicated and most importantly understood by our audiences.

Years ago I worked on a movie set. I had a small non speaking role in the film. I was given the screenplay for my scene in which I was to act. I was kind of surprised that it was really just a few basic pages describing action and character dialogue. I remember thinking that there wasn't much on the page. How do those pages turn into the full drama of a movie? When I got to the movie set there was all this busy commotion and coordination of the director, actors, costume and make-up, set designers, cameramen, and a plethora of other people. They were providing the supporting structure that would eventually transform those few words into a fully realized film magically projected on the silver screen.

A movie, much like a speech, starts with just a basic rough outline. Turning that content into what you eventually see projected in the theatre require a structure that will effectively communicate that content or story to the audience. The director's overall vision for the movie, his core message, is absolutely central to the work and everything must relate back to it cohesively for the movie to "work". The same, as we have already discussed, is also true when putting together a speech. Just as in the movies, everything must be focused on delivering that vision or message as clearly and effectively as intended.

Just like in the movies, a speech needs to have a hook; something that draws you in and creates a sense of curiosity or intrigue. It is this process that answers the audience's question of "what's in it for me?" Think of one of your favorite movies. Isn't it true that within the first few minutes of the movie, the director had already piqued your interest? You want to know what's going to happen. This sets up the structure you end up using because the remainder of the movie, or your speech, will be the resolution of their curiosity through stories, analogies, and points. These then reveal your core message, the lesson, or the moral you're trying to covey.

Good structure is seamless. In fact the best structure is one that is invisible, one that you aren't even aware is there supporting everything. Again simplicity is the option and the one I recommend. You want to avoid a struggle between your content and its structure. If you make the structure complicated, your audience will have a hard time understanding and following the content of your speech. You sometimes see this with movies that have complex storylines. They can be hard to follow especially if it's late and you're tired. The complexity makes it demanding of your attention. But when it comes to a speech, the content should be uncluttered and clear, easy to understand, and flowing logically, after all you want your message to stick. Remember, you're holding the audience's attention, so it's always going to be better to make it easy for them to follow your train of thought.

In his seminal work *Poetics*[15], the Ancient Greek Philosopher Aristotle gave us a basic structural outline of stories. Over two thousand years later, his simple outline is still the bedrock of sound structure. It has been equally applicable to the art of speech-craft as it has been to art of storytelling itself. Aristotle understood that success depended on dividing dramatic narrative into three acts: Act One, the beginning; Act Two, the middle; and Act Three, the end. Pretty simple stuff, yet absolutely essential none the less, proving the old adage that "if it ain't broke don't fix it". You see this simple basic pattern repeated throughout the ages and it is the primary structure still used today. If you listen to or read all the great speeches from throughout the world and all history, you find this same simple logical structure repeated again and again.

Let's look at each Act so see how it breaks down.

- Act One sets up the main character's dilemma, and commits them to resolving it. In a speech, you present the problem that your central premise or core message will resolve or provide a solution for.

- Act Two develops the underlying conflict between the main character and whatever forces stand between him or her and the resolution of the conflict. This is the body of your speech where you explain, expound, and support your core message with stories, anecdotes, analogies, etc.

---

[15] Butcher, S.H. (1902). *The Poetics of Aristotle* (3rd ed.). New York, NY: The Macmillan Company.

- Act Three resolves the conflict and shows us how the character has changed along the way, often hinting at the character's ultimate destiny. In your speech, this is your summation and your strong call to action. How do you want your audience to feel, act, or think differently about as a result of hearing the core message of your speech?

In this section we'll get right into the action of building a speech, discussing all the various parts and elements and the different types of speeches. You'll get the keys that will help unlock structure so that it illuminates your core message letting it shine with bright clarity, moving your audiences by how you say what you say, whatever you choose to say.

Simple and Effective Structure

"That's been one of my mantras - focus and simplicity. Simple can be harder than complex: You have to work hard to get your thinking clean to make it simple. But it's worth it in the end because once you get there, you can move mountains" - Steve Jobs

In the following section we will be looking at the various elements that comprise a sound structure for your speech or presentation. Studying these elements and how they can be effectively incorporated into a speech, you will begin to understand how to make your speech or presentation take form and come alive. Our purpose as speakers is to provide our audiences with clear content communicated and structured in an easy and effective manner, and hopefully presented with some style and panache.

You have probably heard the golden rule of public speaking: tell them what you're going to say, say it, and then tell them what you said - pretty simple. You can see how easily this ties into Aristotle's three acts.

- Act One = What you're going to say
- Act two = Say it
- Act Three = Tell them what you said

This is by far the most effective and by far the simplest way to structure absolutely any speech or presentation. It's unquestionably the most common approach used by all types of speakers all around the world because it works.

I have learned how to structure a speech from trial and error. It can be reduced to the fact that you never really fail until you actually stop trying. Perfecting is a process. Constantly striving at improvement, at the integration of new knowledge and feedback, incrementally builds your confidence. When I was first getting started as a speaker, I struggled with poor structure. I had a propensity for overcomplicating my structure. I'd come up with all these weird, complicated and baffling ways of telling stories. Bizarrely I thought that I was adding intrigue but in truth I was just adding layers of confusion. In retrospect I was actually acting against my own intuition; simplicity just feels better, it's more settled and uncluttered.

Another struggle I had with structure was editing and prioritizing my content. My points always felt rushed and weakly supported because I was cramming way too much information into the speeches. I earnestly wanted to say everything there was to say about my topic. The truth is that you will never be able to say everything there is to say about any topic.

In the previous section we asked questions and gathered all our potential content. Now we must decide what to use and what to leave out, how we will weave it all together so that it is appealing, relatable and understandable to our audience. With fewer well selected points you get more space to incorporate smooth transitions building momentum to your key message.

One of my early speaking mentors explained to me that audiences always want to know where they are going; they want to see a roadmap with all the various stops along the way circled, clearly spelled out and enumerated. It made sense to me because I always want to check a map before I travel. There is a sense of comfort in knowing where you'll be and how you'll get there. Likewise when you provide your audience with a roadmap, it allows them to relax and settle in. They know exactly what's in store for them and when they should expect it, and so they will be enthusiastically willing to come along with you for the duration of your speech, wherever you choose to take them.

Have you ever heard a speech that lacked structure? How could you tell that the problem was with the structure? Oftentimes, we're not quite able to precisely put our fingers on what isn't working in a given speech; rather we just intuitively know that it isn't working. You probably found yourself struggling to follow along. Maybe you started checking your phone, talking to a neighbour, or and your attention starts to waver. Poor structure isn't the only reason you might have felt this way but I have found that it is usually the most obvious culprit.

Creating Connection

"Creativity is the power to connect the seemingly unconnected" - William Plomer

Before you launch into your speech, it is essential that you first create some sort of connection with your audience. In essence you are warming them up and allowing them to settle into their seats and focus their attention on you. This should, at the most, represent about 5% of the total duration of your speech. It's not part of your actual "speech or presentation" rather it is about creating a bit of familiarity. A room always takes a few minutes to settle down as people ease into their seats, get pen and paper, and look you over. Whether they are aware of it or not they are sizing you up. Give them the time they need because the entire audience's attention must be focused on you before you begin your speech otherwise they'll be playing catch up right from the get-go. You are letting them line up at the start line before the race begins.

For a short speech of fifteen minutes or less, you simply stand in the middle of your speaking area, smile and take in the audience. Allow them to focus in on you and quiet down before beginning. It's seems obvious and easy but it is essential to do.

Audience members want to feel acknowledged and a passing glance coupled with a sincere smile will most often do the trick. A glance and smile may seem pretty trivial but they do create connection because you have acknowledged them and given them time to focus in on you.

For presentations of fifteen minutes and up, you'll need to spend a bit more time connecting with the audience - still about 5% of the total duration. Start in the same way as you would for a shorter speech by making sure to make eye contact with the audience and smile!

Then you can establish a bit of rapport by saying a few words about your impressions of the city or town you're in - if you are visiting – but remember to be complimentary. No one wants their home town disrespected, no matter where they live. You can also use this time to acknowledge the organizers by name, recount a short story about something that happened while traveling, or an interesting bit of news from the morning paper that has relevance; there are no rules except that you must keep it light and positive. Remember that you and the audience are getting comfortable with each other and the point of this exercise is for you to be creating a solid connection with the audience. This process humanizes you and reassures the audience that you're friendly and unthreatening and it also goes a long way in creating a sense of unity amongst the members of the audience. They begin to feel that they are part of a single unified whole and that everyone's in this together.

When it comes to workshops or seminars, which are typically longer presentations, you will need to establish a deeper connection and create some group dynamics easily accomplished with a suitable ice breaker exercise. An ice breaker is a short fun exercise where the participants introduce themselves and share a small bit about themselves with the group. A good ice breaker can go a long way in quickly creating a sense of trust and unity; which is an essential quality in establishing good group participation throughout the seminar or workshop.

This getting to know you time is when the audience settles down and nestles into their seats. They begin to focus on you as the speaker and get ready to come along with you for the ride. Remember that it is important to keep your comments and interactions light. Be friendly, smile, and use eye-contact to start building rapport.

Begin with a Bang

"Drama is very important in life: You have to come on with a bang. You never want to go out with a whimper. Everything can have drama if it's done right; Even a pancake" - Julia Child

Being very clear about your speech topic and providing your audience with a detailed roadmap pointing out all the stops ahead is a fundamental basic of any good presentation. However you must also do all you can to grab your audience's attention right away. Beginning with a bang generates interest, curiosity and intrigue. We humans tend to remember most how things begin and end. Those are the two points in a speech that can have the highest impact on audiences. Opening with a bang will grab their attention. They will be titillated, connected, and curious.

Studies have repeatedly shown that your audience's first impressions will usually be forged within the first few seconds of your speech, so don't miss your opportunity to impress them by energetically walking on stage like you own it. As the expression goes, "you only get to make a first impression once", so make it count!

So think about what you can do. Go for something unexpected and interesting that will grab their attention within those first few precious seconds. This can be achieved by asking the audience a thought provoking question or by saying something controversial - be mindful not to offend anyone – or by any other means that creates impact, makes you look good, and is memorable. Some speakers start with a song or a poem. If, and only if, you have a good voice should you even consider singing. The litmus test for singing ability is that someone other than a friend or family member has complemented you on your singing voice. You can also use a poignant quote that sets up your topic or even start with something purely physical to get their attention. Whatever you choose must tie into your topic or message and the connection should be obvious.

Anything normal is boring so think differently and think creatively. Avoid doing the same tired thing that you have seen others do. Predictability doesn't rouse much interest. The mundane is lacklustre. How do you stand out from the crown? The idea here is to create a good solid positive impact with your audience; you want to grab their attention, and get them completely focused.

You will need to think about and determine whether your attention grab is appropriate for your audience. Make sure that you do your homework, ask for advice, and always keep it classy and positive. Present yourself as professional, personable, and confident in your message.

Every year Toastmasters International holds an international competition for the next World Champion of Public Speaking. In 1999, that honour was bestowed on Darren Lacroix, who took the grand prize with his speech "Ouch!" After initially establishing some rapport with audience of over one thousand attendees, Darren recounted the story of his unfortunate Submarine Shop failure. Less than a minute in, he stumbles and falls flat on his face – literally with a loud thump – and then proceeded to stay down for so long that the audience became visibly uncomfortable. Then when the tension was at its height he raised his head and addressed the audience, still flat on the ground, asking them, "Have you ever fallen flat on your face?" Brilliant - It has been said that that was the precise moment when Darren won the competition and coveted title of World Champion of Public Speaking. Learn from this world champ and do the unexpected by opening your speech with a bang.

Tell'em What You're Going to Tell'em

Ok so now that you have created a strong connection with the audience by opening with a bang, what comes next? Well, put yourself squarely in the shoes of your audience, they want to know where you will be taking them with your speech. Most of all, they want to know "what's in it for me". You can put them at ease by giving them a clear and simple overview of what you will be covering during the speech.

As a speaker it is your job and your responsibility to make sure that your audiences always have a clear and well-articulated roadmap to follow. You must introduce your topic, give a basic overview of your key message and enumerate the various major points that you will be making. In this way the audience can mentally prepare themselves for what is coming. It allows them to remain with you as you weave them through your speech peppering the points of your presentation with stories, analogies, and all your other content.

Tell'em

Once you have created that vital connection with your audience, and you've grabbed their attention and told them what you're going to say, go ahead and say what you have to say.

Remember to stick strictly to your theme or message. If you can't relate the information back to your theme, point, or message your audience won't be able to do so either. Don't lose or confuse them. Sticking to your points and seeing them through to the end will guarantee good communication.

Ask yourself some probing questions:

- Why am I doing this action or activity?
- Why am I choosing to say this in this way?
- Is this relevant to my theme or point?
- Am I providing too much information?
- Am I proving too little information?
- Is this clear?

How you choose to structure your information will depend on the duration of your speech, its purpose, and who your intended audience will be. That being said, there are a few tips, tools, and techniques that will work in just about any presentation to keep you on track and moving forward. The following will greatly help you define, polish, and organize your speech's content.

The Rule of Three

The Latin phrase *"omne trium perfectum"* (everything that comes in threes is perfect) is an ancient source of the rule of three and illustrates how deeply the rule is rooted in our collective conscious. This is not some modern spin, it is a perceptual fact. In the art of writing, there is a very well-accepted standard that states that all things that come in threes are funnier, more complete and much more satisfying to the listener. Triads of three words or three ideas combine both brevity and rhythm while providing the smallest amount of information needed to create a pattern. Additionally it gives you, the speaker, the appearance of being knowledgeable while remaining simple, clear and catchy. And triads also function as potent mnemonic devices allowing for both the audience and speaker to more readily recall words and thus ideas.

Effective use of the triad is indispensable to public speaking. Organizing your content into three main points will give your presentations the appearance of being more polished, complete and satisfying. In fact, this book has been organized along those very same principles with the information being presented in the form of three main subject headings – Content, Structure, and Delivery. The rule of three is equally important whether it's a five minute speech or a multiple day presentation event. Intellectually, it just makes things easier for our brains to relate to, remember and recall.

But what if you have more than three point that you want to discuss? The simple answer is that each of your main three points can be subsequently divided into three smaller points again and again. Ultimately, you can parcel an awful lot of information this way. Try to stick to the structure of the rule of three when structuring your presentations and they will be more complete and memorable.

A Few Good Words

A short speech, less than fifteen minutes in duration, should always have a crystal clear singular theme or point thoroughly expressed in just a few well-chosen words. If you are delivering a longer presentation, workshop, or seminar, not only must you have your theme narrowed to a few succinct words, but each of your main points should likewise be crafted into a foundational phrase that encapsulates your various points.

For Example:

Theme
- Goals - The Gateway to Your Dreams

1st Point
- Figuring out what you really want

2nd Point
- Set a plan and put it in motion

3rd Point
- Stay the course to the finish line

Each point must relate to your overall theme and be an elaboration of one of its aspects. It is crucial that you be able to state your point clearly in one short sentence of a dozen words or less. This is a very important structural step that will help you get focused, categorize and develop your content.

Getting your ideas down to twelve words or less can be a bit challenging especially if those concepts you're conveying seem to be a bit complex. However, remember that if you yourself are having trouble being clear and succinct - by getting your point down to a short simple phrase – then you can pretty much guarantee that your audience will be struggling too. If you are having difficulty narrowing down your points, start by asking yourself plenty of questions about your content, always narrowing it down to the concentrate, and then do some more developmental work to get that elusive clarity. Put on your thinking cap and fine tune and focus your point until you get a handle on it and work it down to a few well-chosen words as in the example given above. Remember that if you, the speaker, are unable to be brief, focused and clear in conveying the theme of your topic, it will be virtually impossible for any audience to follow along.

Once you have your points whittled down to just a dozen words or so, practice a little "word-smithing" by making those words as catchy and sticky as you can. Here are a few things to consider when creating your foundational phrase. Find an internal rhythm, rhyme or alliteration within the phrase so that it sticks in the mind when it is heard. The easier it is to repeat, the more easily remembered.

Here are a few examples to help you get the idea:

- Practice makes perfect
- Pay what you owe, and you're worth you will know
- The more you put in, the more you get out
- If you love life, life will love you back
- Don't just tell them, sell them
- Life doesn't require that we be the best, only that we try our best

These short pithy phrases easily convey their meaning and stick like glue to the mind. A well-crafted phrase is more readily remembered long after your presentation is over, especially if you repeat the phrase several times throughout your presentation. Don't be afraid to play around with words and be as creative as you dare with how you phrase your points, remembering that it is always wiser to select simple words that have a clear and unambiguous meaning, that sound solid together - and where possible – words that have an internal rhyme and rhythm.

Think of this exercise as the purposeful concentration of your content, all those ideas and impressions about your topic, point or message into mighty little packages. Do this and your speeches will soon sparkle. They will sound more polished, more professional, and best of all they will be easily remembered and repeated.

The Roadmap

When designing and delivering a longer presentation, workshop, or seminar it is absolutely imperative that you provide your audience with a clear roadmap as we have already discussed. Audiences want to know where you will be taking them and what they should expect and anticipate from you and your presentation. A roadmap makes them aware of all the stops you'll be pointing out throughout the journey.

Imagine you signed up for a bus tour of an unfamiliar city you are visiting. The tour guide says nothing about where he's taking you, how long it will take, or what you'll see along the way. He just takes off without warning. So there you are on a bus to God-knows-where, you have no idea how long you'll be gone or what to expect. How comfortable would you feel? How confident would you be in the tour guide?

If you're like most people, you'd have a few apprehensions. Chances are you'd be anxious and unimpressed not knowing the destinations or how long you'd be gone. You'd find it pretty tough to simply kick back and relax. That uneasy feeling would steal your enjoyment of the experience. The same is true when it comes to a speech, and even more so, when it comes to longer presentations. Roadmaps are absolutely vital.

So audiences want to know where they are going. It helps them settle in, feel safe and relax. Roadmaps also whet an audience's appetite. It's like a detailed description of a delicious dish on a menu. It helps you visualize and even crave what is coming. So a good roadmap should create a bit of anticipation, give the audience something to look forward to, and allow them to have complete clarity.

Keep it simple and clear. Your objective is to provide clarity not confusion, so try not to have more than three main points and don't give them too much information about any of the points up front. Remember you are creating a roadmap with only the main attractions. There are many different ways to create great roadmaps that are simple, clear, and most importantly, highly effective.

Here are a few Roadmap suggestions:

- **Use an acronym**
  The 3 D's of Effective email management. (Do, Delegate, or Delete)
- **Number your points**
  One, Two, Three, Etc
- **State each point at the beginning**
  Effective Management - Time, People, and Resources
- **Create a metaphorical landscape**
  Project Management – Navigating your Landscape
- **Provide a handout or an agenda**

As you can see from the above suggestions, creating a roadmap doesn't have to be cumbersome or complicated, in fact if your roadmap is simple and clear your audiences will appreciate knowing that you know where you're going and that you have everything under control and they'll have confidence in you.

Done well, a roadmap is a powerful way of also projecting confidence as a speaker, creating immediate audience buy-in, and displaying your professionalism and your sense of organization. With your audiences riveted and sitting on the edge of their seats, they'll be happy and enthusiastic to follow you wherever you choose to take them.

For shorter speeches, your roadmap should be a little less formal or fussy. It should simply be covered by your topic introduction: the part of the speech where you tell them what you are going to tell them. However, the roadmap is an absolutely necessity with lengthy presentations.

Making your Point

"You were born to win, but to be a winner, you must plan to win, prepare to win, and expect to win" - Zig Ziglar

Now that you have focused your points into the well selected words of a foundational phrase and you are clear about what you want to say, it's time to delve into your content and simply put - say it. This is the part of your speech or presentation where you want to make the "big sale". You want to convince your audience, sell them on your point of view, and change their thinking, behaviour, or values as a result. In essence you're telling them the point of your point!

A powerful approach in making your point, and one that I would highly recommend, is to make your point by presenting a problem, dilemma or conflict at first – one that the audience can easily relate to - and resolving it with your recommended solution. This makes your points the solutions to their problems. In storytelling, the problem arises out of the conflict, which must then come to a climax, with the resolution revealed as the moral of the story.

You will have a much stronger and a more lasting impact on your audiences if the point you are making is seen as the solution to a problem they can identify with. With this technique, they will more readily remember your points and they will easily be able to put your points into practice.

This can be accomplished in several different ways:

- Use facts or stats as your support
- Use the compare and/or contrast approach
- Use analogies or metaphors
- Illustrate your point through a story
- Use a powerful or poignant quote
- Ask probing, powerful, or provocative questions

Facts

We've looked at presenting facts and figures, charts, and graphs above but let's refresh our memories and have another look. If you are going to use facts, do so sparingly. You will find very few audience members that get excited or riveted by the mere mention of facts and stats. Less is more. Rather than listing a long litany of numbers and figures, go for effect and impact. Keep in mind that you only want the facts to support and illustrate your point and that those facts must be presented in a relatable way.

Explain what they mean or what is implied by the facts and make sure to always provide your sources. If you are going to use facts or statistics to support your point, you yourself must fully understand them first, what they mean, and the implications of the provided information. The last thing you want is for an audience member to question the legitimacy of the fact you are using as support for your point.

Compare and Contrast

Another great way of supporting your point is to use the compare and contrast methodology. In this method you illustrate the positive aspects of following the advice and guidance of your message while contrasting it with the negative aspects of not following that advice and guidance making sure that the preferred and proscribed choice is absolutely obvious.

This can be accomplished by contrasting two stories that have parallel elements where one is a positive example to follow while the other is a negative example to be avoided. Done well, the compare and contrast methodology will illuminate a stark contrast that will sell your point of view as the right one to adopt. Be mindful that the two things, approaches or stories being compared are similar enough in outline and circumstances that they can be correlated effectively. Additionally, you will want a sufficient degree of contrast between the two principles being compared to illustrate, without any doubt, that your point is the better approach.

Analogies and Metaphors

When talking about something that is complex or hard to imagine, analogies and metaphors can be life-savers. In using analogies and metaphors, you connect your ideas to something that the audience already knows, understands, and can readily relate to. When trying to find a suitable analogy or metaphor to help convey your meaning, ask yourself, "What is this like? What does this remind me of?" By creating an association between something well known and familiar with something that is a bit more complex or esoteric, analogies and metaphors help your audience's understand. That being said the topic doesn't necessarily have to be complex in order for you to use a metaphor or analogy. They work in just about any situation where clarity and deeper understandability are key to your message. When used with purpose, analogies and metaphors have the potential to also infuse an emotional connection, some humour, additional relevance, or more by-in to your point of view. Additionally they can give you the opportunity to infuse colourful language and vivid imagery making your speech sound a bit more poetical. All great speakers are masters of this tool and use it liberally to great effect.

Stories

Nothing is more powerful to our mind than a well recounted story with all its drama, conflict, climax, and concluding message. We remember and describe almost everything that happens and that we witness in our lives in terms of stories. We all recount our lives and experiences though stories, we see ourselves and all we do as stories and stories are at the heart of every other person and thing we know.

No matter what the speech type that you are delivering - its length, topic or intended audience - you will never ever go wrong using one or more stories to substantiate and elaborate your points. Stories don't necessarily have to be long or complicated in structure for them to create strong connections with your audiences. We humans are all preprogrammed to go along for the ride as soon as we hear a story. Our affinity is deeply rooted in human condition. We're curious by nature and so we always want to know what's going to happen in the end; how the story will turn out after all the twists and turns.

Stories animate and enliven the points you are making in your speech and bring them into focus. A great story, well told, will have your audience sitting on the edge of their seats completely enraptured. Stories may well be the basic nuts and bolts of public speaking but your audiences can always tell if you are simply re-telling a story or whether you are reliving it. It's a very important distinction that we must make when we recount our tales. As a speaker you can only really re-live your very own personal stories, those experiences that you have actually struggled or triumphed through; because you have lived through them, they provide the multi-dimensionality of experience for an authentic re-telling of the drama. Whereas when you simply re-tell someone else's story, you end up losing some of the emotional depth and the multi-dimensionality of a felt and lived experience. So, personal stories are always the best stories to share.

Remember that you, and you alone, are in control of your own personal stories, so if you are sheepish or have apprehensions about sharing certain particulars of your tale, simply steer clear. If for some reason you are still dealing with the strong and unsettled emotions of any given experience - if it's just too raw - simply steer clear. The audience should not be used as your personal therapist and no one wants to see you have an emotional breakdown live on the platform. You only have to share what you are willing to share and no more than that. You are in control.

It's also beneficial to remember this key point: an audience always pictures themselves, and not you, as the characters in the recounting of your story. You too have had this experience as an attendee; the narrator gives details that you then see through your very own eyes as though you were the one living the experiences retold in the story. This is after all the basis for catharsis. We experience it whenever we hear a story. We picture ourselves squarely in the action and characters of the story be it as victor, hero, or even as villain. So if you're going to tell a story, try to make it your own through its re-living. Making it both personal and purposeful are the two key aspects of storytelling success.

Your story doesn't have to be grand and awe striking. It's not necessary for you to have climbed Everest, survived a near death experience, or to be a superstar of some sort for your personal story to have a strong and meaningful message. The mundane everyday experiences are just as valuable and instructive if you have a good point to make through the telling. The purpose of a story is in conveying a message that is held within the drama or tragedy, the efficacy of the story is found in making that point come to life.

Quotes

A good quote can go a long way towards adding a sense of credibility or authority to the points you are trying to make through your speech. Through the use of a quote you are, in essence, providing your audience with a verifiable and trusted source or authority who is in agreement and alignment with your particular point of view. A quote also gives you the opportunity to infuse some humour or wit into your speech through the words of another. Quotes are important and interesting adjuncts to any speech. They add colour. One of my favorite authors to quote is Oscar Wilde. He is always a worthy choice when it comes to humorous wit. I have read him, know his biographical details, and so I am very comfortable quoting him. You can't go wrong with him especially if wit is what you are looking for.

- *There are only two tragedies in life: one is not getting what one wants, and the other is getting it* - Oscar Wilde[16]

- *Experience is simply the name we give our mistakes* – Oscar Wilde[17]

Find an authority that resonates with you, one that you know something about, and that will be known and respected by your audience. If the person quoted is lesser known, give the audience a few biographical details so that they can relate better.

Ex: Oscar Wilde was a late nineteenth century poet, playwright, and most famously the author of *The Picture of Dorian Gray*.

A few words of caution; avoid using over quoted material that is too familiar and that everyone has heard a million times over. Those quotes have lost most of their punch, they have become overly predictable, and they are obvious and maybe even a little dull. Only use them if you have something interesting and unexpected to say about them.

When choosing a quote don't just use a quote without knowing at least something about the author, you don't need to be an expert but you should know some basic biographical facts about the authority and the work that the quote was extracted from. Believe me it can be very embarrassing to have an audience member come up to you after your speech and want to talk to you about the authority you just quoted during your speech only for them to

---

[16] Oscar Wilde. (1998). *Oscar Wilde's Wit and Wisdom: A Book of Quotations.* Mineola, NY: Dover Publications.

[17] Oscar Wilde. (1998). *Oscar Wilde's Wit and Wisdom: A Book of Quotations.* Mineola, NY: Dover Publications.

discover that you know precious little about the author nor the subject matter being quoted.

Years ago, I used a quote that was wholly unfamiliar to me from an authority that I knew nearly nothing about. After I delivered my speech, an eager member of the audience, who loved the author and was very well versed, waited patiently to speak to me on the subject of the quoted author for over twenty minutes only to discover that I had merely copied and pasted the quote from the internet. To my embarrassment, I knew nearly nothing about the author or his seminal works. I simply smiled in my ignorance blushing in my humiliation. It is a mistake that I have never allowed myself to repeat.

Another important point to keep in mind is that you should never quote someone without giving them full due credit, no matter who is being quoted be it a friend, family, or boss. Using quoted material without sourcing is tantamount to plagiarism and someone in the audience will always know and potentially call you out.

Avoid the embarrassment and make it a rule of thumb to always cite the authority behind your quotes and also give due credit for any material that you are using that is not your intellectual property. In most instances its fine to use other peoples material as long as you give its creator full due credit unless there are copyright issues to consider.

Questions

Questions are another absolutely essential tool that should be sharpened and added to every presenter's toolkit. They can give you an instant connection to any audience because it is virtually impossible to hear a question without immediately answering that question in your head. For example, what did you have for breakfast today? What is you favorite colour? How old are you? If you are like most people, you began to ponder a response as soon as you read the questions. Just asking the question elicits a response. It's as if our minds are on auto-pilot and when we hear a question and we are simply pre-programed to reply whether out loud or in merely in our own heads. For a speaker, this is very powerful stuff when used expertly.

A great way to get immediate audience engagement is to start your speech with a well-crafted question as a touch stone and introduction to your topic. You'll get the audience thinking and engaged in your topic right away, they will start to anticipate a resolution or a suitable answer to the question you asked, and they will all be focused on the same thing.

The question can be a provocative one, especially if you are trying to shake some pre-held assumptions or notions that the audience holds Vis a Vis a certain topic.

Ex: Did you know that you're body is only worth about $160? That's right: if you bought all the raw minerals that make up a human body such as Water, Oxygen, Carbon, Potassium, etc. that's all you'd have to pay. So how do we measure the worth of a person?

As you can see from the above example, the question can also be used as a bit of a misleader meant to elicit surprise or shock when your point of view is finally revealed. This type of question helps to make your point more memorable.

When possible, use open-ended questions. They are much more engaging and thought provoking and will always generate more and deeper reflection. Open-ended questions are questions that generally start with who, what, why, where, when and how; whereas closed questions will generally only get you a "yes" or "no" response. Know what you want the audience to think and ask the right questions in order to steer the audience in that direction.

When asking a question, remember that you are trying to build a positive connection or rapport with your audience, so make sure that you are respectful and tactful in what and how you ask your questions.

As was stated above, we automatically reply to questions in our heads so be mindful to give the audience enough time to respond to the question in their minds. Ask your question and then count 2-5 seconds in your head, before you continue. A small pause should suffice.

And finally, questions can above all be powerful tools for inducing self-reflection in an audience. A well-timed and well-worded question can help you direct your audience by inviting them to think more deeply about certain issues in preparation for the information that you will be imparting. Likewise, when appropriate, a well-crafted question will always be effective in getting the audience on the same "topic" page, or in getting them to remember a past event, or even in imagining the possibilities of what might be. Questions create connections quickly so use them to your advantage.

A Final Word on Tools

In the end whatever tools you choose to use to help you make your point, they must be effective. Always be mindful that any tool overused loses its sharpness and becomes dull and blunt quickly losing its intended effect. Anything that is overused tends to become gimmicky and a bit cliché. Permit yourself the use of only a few of these tools for a short speech – perhaps just a story, some facts and a few good questions – however for longer presentations you will want to vary the tools you use for each point that you are making. Don't be afraid to shake it up and use a variety of these tools in your speeches as a way of keeping your audiences interested and engaged in your topic. Put yourself in the audience's shoes to gauge their level of interest and interaction and then use these tools to make it pop.

The Recap and Transition

"Instead of worrying about what people say of you, why not spend time trying to accomplish something they will admire" – Dale Carnegie

For longer presentations, such as keynotes, workshops, and seminars that contain several different points or segments, a subject or segment recap is essential in keeping your audiences on the same page as you and for reviewing the most important elements as a way of ensuring that the meaning of your message is being understood for the entire duration of your talk. This is particularly true if you are building an argument as you go through the presentation. If the audiences misses any one part that you are presenting they may become confused about everything that comes next.

A great way to avoid this is to ensure that before transitioning from one point to another, you use the recap as an opportunity to reinforce your point, check for comprehension, and to provide an opportunity for questions if appropriate. In fact the recap can often be a great time for getting audience participation in helping them fill in the blanks, for example, "so the three D's of time management are…?" or "therefore it is better to give that to____?" You can cup your ear with your hand to indicate to the audience that this is not a rhetorical exercise and that you want them to speak up. Whenever you are able to get the audience to repeat your words, they'll sink deeper and will subsequently become more memorable.

If you have used a foundational phrase of a dozen words or less and you have repeated them throughout your presentation, you could ask the audience to repeat the words back to you in your recap. This is what is referred to as a *call and response* technique and it is highly effective for establishing a strong understanding, audience participation, and deeper learning. In using a recap, you are reinforcing learning and drilling in the message you want them to walk away with.

You can also have a brief discussion and debrief about the point you have just made. This can be a bit tricky to control in terms of time and should be well planned. Anytime you get the audience involved in a discussion, you are relinquishing a portion of the control of your presentation, you open yourself up to the possibility of someone saying something irrelevant or off-colour, or going off on an irrelevant tangent. You should always know exactly how you'll bring the audience back to attention – by clapping hands, a buzzer, or bell – and you should always tell the audience how much time will be allocated to the discussion or debrief. Use a stopwatch to keep on track and let the audience know when only one minute remains so that they can start wrapping up the discussion and start refocusing on you. It can be a bit tricky and should be well planned. This technique is better suited to a speaker who has some experience in moderating discussions and who has the ability to bring the discussion to a satisfactory close within the allotted time. Once the time is up, restate the main points in a brief sentence that encapsulates the discussion, making sure that you tie it in with the points or message that you were making in the previous section.

Recaps and transitions are in many ways similar to mini-conclusions, however they differ in one very significant way, a good recap should also incorporate a bit of a teaser of what is coming next in your presentation. Create anticipation in the audience by wetting their appetite and creating interest. Not only are you restating your mains points but you are also using this opportunity to sell the audience on what is coming up next. The recap, when done well, is an effective way of holding their attention.

Transitioning from one point to another, from story to story, or from one section of a speech to another - no matter how long the speech may be - is absolutely instrumental to maintaining a good forward flow to your speeches and for ensuring that the audience remains with you all the way through.

Have you ever been an audience member when all of a sudden you realize that the speaker has moved onto another subject yet you had no idea where or when that had happened? Obviously the transition from one subject to another was ineffective. The ensuing result being that you got confused, lost, and disoriented. Transitions should always be smooth but above all else undeniably obvious.

The effective use of a recap and subsequent promise of what's coming next make it obvious to your audiences that you have finished one part of your talk and that you are now transitioning to another part of your talk. We will look at ways of using your stage presence and movements to additionally aide with creating strong, smooth, and obvious transitions in the delivery section of this book.

Call to Action

"When dealing with people, remember you are not dealing with creatures of logic, but creatures of emotion" – Dale Carnegie

Whenever you are presenting a motivational or inspirational speech, you must have a very strong call to action that grabs your audience's attention and persuades them to follow your recommendation enthusiastically. Although you will need a strong call to action under these circumstances, you should always incorporate a call to action regardless of the type of speech or presentation that you are delivering. If you miss this important opportunity, you will come across as a bit wishy-washy or indecisive to your audience.

Ask yourself this key question: What do you want your audience to do differently as a result of your speech?

Whether you want them to act, think or feel differently, your call to action should clearly state your objective in a very clear and compelling way. The call to action is an explicit appeal to your audience to take a specific course of action following your speech. After all, this is the inherent purpose of your persuasive, inspirational, informational, or motivational speech. Although a strong call to action is most forcefully used in persuasive, inspirational or motivational speeches, it must also be appropriately used in any type of speech.

The call to action speaks to your purpose. Why are you telling your audience what you are telling them? What do you want to accomplish as a result of your advice and guidance? How do you want them to act, think, or feel differently once you have concluded?

Here are a few key principles to keep in mind. Your call to action should...

- **Be clear and direct**
  Use strong bold clear and commanding language. It is a call to action not a suggestion to action.

- **Get them to take action right away**
  The longer it takes to initiate the action, the more likely that your audience will lose motivation. Procrastination is the killer of dreams so if they can do something before they leave the

room that is best. Remember that the longer the delay, the weaker the action taken.

- **Make it easy for them to do**
  To help your audience act quickly, eliminate as many barriers to action as you can and make sure to always be positive and supportive in tone.

- **Focus on the benefits**
  Always frame your call-to-action in the audience's best interest while remaining realistic. Eliminate as many excuses as possible.

- **Make it you (audience) focused**
  Address the individual, not the group. You must establish a personal connection.

Tell them what you told them

"If everyone is moving forward together, then success takes care of itself." – Henry Ford

When it comes to conclusions, like recaps and transitions, they should be obvious. The audience must know and feel that you are wrapping things up. Keep in mind that the most memorable part of your speech or presentation will always be the beginning and the end; the end being a bit more impressed in the audience's mind that the beginning. It is well researched and documented that we tend to remember most what we have heard last, so make sure that you don't waste this most valuable and important opportunity to make an impact – it's time to restate all your main points while tying them all up into your theme.

Your conclusion is where all the various parts points, stories and messages of your speech should come together in perfect harmony. Creating a clear sense of completion is important for obvious reasons; you don't want your audience to walk away from your presentation with a feeling that something important is missing, or that your speech was incomplete or incoherent.

It's ok for them to have questions inspired by or arising from your speech topic, however you don't want them to walk away questioning your purpose or what your points were all about and how they relate to them. Your conclusion must always tie the content of your main points to your overarching theme with a strong clear call to action as we discussed above.

In fact, you can maximize the impact of your conclusion by using it to really reinforce the transfer of learning by encouraging your audience to participate in the conclusion by getting them to restate your main points through a "call and answer" or a "fill-in the blanks" activity. You can infuse a lot of fun with these types of activities but you must remember to always keep it simple. Cup your ear with your hand to indicate to the audience that you want them to participate by answering out loud.

A key point to consider and to remember at all times is that the activity shouldn't be what I refer to as "stump the chump". Rather as the speaker, you should do everything in your power to set your audience up for success by keeping the answers to your questions as simple and obvious as possible so that everybody will readily know that answer. The purpose is not to make them sweat though some stress-filled test or examination; it's really about reinforcing your message by getting them to repeat the information that you told them previously. If you make the audience work too hard to succeed in this activity or if you make the questions too complicated or esoteric, you'll end up hearing lots of crickets, the audience will avoid your gaze, hold their heads down, and clam up in silence. So set them up for success by making the answers as obvious as you can and your audiences will be eager to participate. Remember that we all tend to hesitate answering questions when we are unsure of the right answer. If your intension is to get participation make the answers blaringly obvious. After all no one ever wants to look stupid.

SPEAK LIKE A PRO

Part 3

Delivery

"A person, who never made a mistake, never tried anything new" - *Albert Einstein*

Good delivery is a lot like putting the sizzle in the steak – that mystical thing that creates a "wow" factor in any speech. A good speech or presentation should always have some "wow" factor making it more enjoyable, memorable and meaningful to the audience. There isn't any mystery or mystique to a good presentation. You don't have to be born an exuberant extrovert, charmingly charismatic, or be a naturally gifted orator to do well as a speaker.

Obviously it's helpful if you do have some of these qualities to begin with, however every professional public speaker worth their weight in gold has worked very hard to develop and polish their delivery and platform skills. This is something that you too can do so rest assured and take courage because good delivery can indeed be learned and developed with guidance and through practice. Let's have a look at some of the components of delivery.

Gestures

"There are four ways, and only four ways, in which we have contact with the world. We are evaluated and classified by these four contacts: what we do, how we look, what we say, and how we say it" - Dale Carnegie

Public speaking is an audio visual experience for an audience, yet it is easy to forget the visual aspect of a presentation. Aside from the use of projection such as PowerPoint, most people don't usually pay much attention to the visual aspect of speaking, but while the audience is listening attentively to your words they are likewise looking at your body language and gestures, which also communicate something to the audience. In fact, when properly employed, body language greatly expands, reaffirms, and substantiates your words.

This is something that I desperately needed to learn when I first started speaking in public. For example, while speaking to audiences, I'd often shake my head from side to side; the standard visual indication for no or a negative. The problem was that I would be saying the complete opposite. I was saying yes while shaking my head to say no. Of course I was doing this subconsciously. One day a member of the audience approached me to tell me of the incongruity of what I was doing. Nobody had ever mentioned it before and I was a bit skeptical in fact I was completely flabbergasted by the comment and my defenses went straight up. With the obvious insecurity of my novelty to speaking my immediate reaction was denial.

I decided to videotape the speech in its entirety, just to prove to myself that I was doing it right and nodding appropriately to mirror my words. To my horror and embarrassment, I discovered that the audience member had been correct. In fact, I soon saw that there were other physical gestures that I was using that didn't correspond to my spoken words.

In truth, I had never given gestures or body language much thought. I had been almost exclusively focused on the selection of my words, working hard on the language that I employed, and on the ideas and stories that I was expounding. Suddenly, I realized that there was a whole lot more to this speaking business, and so I started paying much closer attention to how I used my body as I spoke and I started recording myself every time I spoke without exception. I would isolate a particular gesture that I was dissatisfied with and then work hard to transform it into what I wanted to project.

I looked at successful speakers in order to get inspired and to see how they incorporated gestures into their speaking style and more importantly I wanted to learn how they were doing it successfully. I'm not suggesting that you imitate your favorite speaker because the best thing you've got going for yourself as a speaker is your authenticity and originality, both impossible to achieve when you're merely copying someone else. Your gestures should be natural to you - what you normally do in normal circumstances - only they should be done with a clear purpose, good timing, and some style. As I focused on perfecting my delivery, I elicited lots and lots of critical feedback from friends, family, and audiences alike. To this day I still record, review, and rework my presentations looking to constantly improve my delivery and the synchronicity of my words and gestures. This is a technique that will keep you improving over time. I highly recommend that you record yourself. I can be a bit tough to watch yourself a first but it will pay in dividends.

Here are a few things to keep in mind when it comes to using gestures effectively:

- **Synchronize your gestures to your words**

    As we have already discussed your words and your gesture must mutually support and reflect each other.

- **Be natural and authentic**
  Move the way you would normally and naturally do and avoid being overly dramatic. Try not to be too self-conscious.

- **Exaggerate your gestures**
  Be yourself but slightly exaggerated. The larger the audience, the larger your gestures should be. In small rooms keep them smaller.

- **Compliment your words, don't compete with them**
  Don't be too distracting in your gestures. You are not a stage actor. Subtlety goes a long way. If your gestures are competing with what you say, try toning them down a bit.

- **Be appropriate to your topic and audience**
  When presenting a very formal or solemn address, your gestures should be extremely minimal. When speaking to young kids you can literally go wild and they will love you for it!

Eye Contact

"The eyes are the windows to the soul" – William Shakespeare

An absolutely essential ingredient for connecting with any other person and particularly with an audience is through the judicious use of eye contact. We gauge each other's sincerity, trustworthiness, and honesty through the eyes as much or more as anything else. Eye contact might seem simple enough at first - you just need to look at someone - however there are methods that can and should be used to maximize the benefits of effective eye contact. You must understand that with poor eye contact you might come across as untrustworthy, as if you're unsure of yourself or you've got something to hide. On the other hand stare at anyone for too long and you'll likely come across as a bit creepy or even menacing.

As is the case with so many other things, the middle path is often the right path to follow – neither overly favouring one nor the other - rather striving for the middle ground combination of both. Good eye contact is a bit of a mixed bag. So much is conveyed through the eyes that we must make sure that our eye contact, like gestures, is congruent with the intent of what we are saying and the feeling we want to project to our audience. The eyes truly are the windows to our souls.

Whether addressing an audience of only ten or numbered in the thousands, each audience member *should feel* as though you have acknowledged them personally. They all want to feel significant and that they matter to you. It is largely through this crucial acknowledgement that you will make that personal connection. The good news is that effective eye contact is simple to do once it is understood.

Just a little glance, a passing over with your eyes if you will, is all that is really required for that connection to begin to take place. You're just trying to communicate this simple sentiment, "Hey, I see you out there, you're important to me and yes I am speaking to you". Couple that glance with a warm smile and you'll have extended a gracious invitation for them to trust you and to listen to what you have to say.

When speaking in a large room with a larger audience, obviously you won't be able to look at everyone individually – it just isn't realistic nor is it necessary. In these situations all you need to do is slowly zigzag your eyes from the very back of the room to the front row while taking in as much of the audience as possible. Glancing a few times back and forth from side to side will suffice. Be smooth in your movement and remember to smile.

This is what you're trying to accomplish: the audience only needs to "feel" that you have seen and acknowledged them – remember that it's all about the audience and how they feel (WIIFM) – so make sure they feel your acknowledgment. Don't ever jilt or ignore them. They'll return the favour by ignoring you in return – after all that's exactly how they feel you are treating them when you don't make adequate eye contact.

A Passing Glance

As discussed above, a good rule of thumb that many speakers employ is the "zigzag survey", where one scans the audience in a zigzag fashion from the back left to back right, middle left to middle right, then to the front left to front right. This should be performed as naturally as possible. You don't want to be robotic or overly obvious in your movements. The purpose is to survey and acknowledge the entire audience – even those in the cheap seats way at the back of the room. Don't rest your eyes on any given individual, rather keep your gaze fluid and in motion. Each member of the audience, no matter where they are seated, should feel that you have connected with them, even if only very briefly. The audience must feel that you have seen them.

Speak to One, Connect to All

An interesting thing happens when our eyes connect with those of an audience member. When our eyes linger, the connection we share with the individual audience member goes deeper and you both feel the depth of the connection when it's done right. This may be somewhat obvious to you however the really interesting aspect of this lingering is that the other members of the audience will feel that they too are connecting with you on a deeper level. How can this be? After all you were only looking at one individual. The answer is that the other members of the audience are connecting with you vicariously; as though they were actually sitting in the place of the person that you are connecting with. As a result of this vicarious effect they feel that you are also connecting with them personally.

This is a very powerful and important process to be aware of as a speaker because it allows you to speak to one and connect to them all. It is an indispensable tool for connecting to your entire audience on a deeper level.

There is a quintessential line between connecting through your eyes with a slight lingering regard and staring at someone or ogling them. If you look at anyone for too long, they will become uneasy and uncomfortable.

When I conduct speaking skills or presentation workshops, I often illustrate this point by staring at an audience member for too long. Within ten to twenty seconds they invariably start to blush. So the trick is to look at them, have them acknowledge that connection by looking back, keep it locked for one two seconds and then move on. You can come back to them again, while still discussing the same point, but do not hold the gaze for too long. This technique is very effective when you are saying something important that you want the audience to pay particular attention to, like when you are delivering a point of wisdom or asking them a question. Do this repeatedly to single audience members throughout your speech to maintain that connection to them all.

There is a time when holding the gaze of an audience member for longer than a few short seconds can be very effective. It can be used when you want to invite an audience member into what I call the "required response" territory, where the audience member is invited to reply, respond or say something out loud. If you are asking a non-rhetorical question – a question that requires an audible response – simply hold your gaze on an audience member that seems eager to answer and remember to smile. Again, be mindful that you are not making someone who is reluctant or shy feel uncomfortable. If they seem adamant about remaining silent, simply move on or look for a volunteer. You never want to drag your audience members when they are clearly resistant. They will rarely forgive your insensitivity nor will the rest of audience.

Many speakers make prior arrangements with specific audience members – known in the industry as plants – as a way to avoid the potential discomfort or derailment of non-responsiveness audiences. Experience has taught me that simply selecting an audience member who seems eager to respond – often seated right up front and on the edge of their seats - elicits a much more natural and spontaneous response and perceived as more authentic to everyone else in the room. This does require a certain level of confidence developed through platform and presentation experience. If you are unsure and need to feel more comfortable and a greater degree of control, a "plant" is absolutely acceptable. The point is that you, the speaker, should always be in control of the presentation. You may want to try to get engagement more naturally and arranging a "plant" just in case they are needed.

I have had, like most speakers, the misfortune of being sabotaged and sidetracked by an overzealous audience member wanting to take over and present a speech in my place. As they say, there's one in every crowd. It soon became very uncomfortable and I could feel the audience looking at me with expectation, as if they were saying, "hey buddy, you'd better do something fast". Finally, in desperation, I invited the audience to join me in applauding and drowning him out. He got the message. I thanked and started right into my next point without looking at the member again for a few minutes.

A scenario like that can be challenging to deal with. Regaining control of a sidetracked presentation is tough. That's where experience, if you have any, typically kicks in. On that particular occasion, early in my speaking career, a plant might not have been such a bad idea. Thankfully, I somehow managed to muddle my way out of it in the end. You must choose and plan your method of audience engagement. If you're quick witted on your feet, comfortable, and experienced then you should have nothing to worry about.

So when it comes to making good eye contact; make sure that you connect with the entire audience with smooth zigzag scanning; create a deeper connection with one audience member and in doing so invite the entire audience to participate vicariously; and connect even more deeply with a focused question to one.

The Pregnant Pause

"The right word may be effective, but no word was ever as effective as a rightly timed pause." – Mark Twain

What is it that makes music, music? When I ask my audiences this quirky question I invariably get the typical responses such as; the notes, sound, instruments, etc... Although those are all true to some extent, very few people ever come up with the answer that I'm looking for – silence. That's probably because it seems counter intuitive, after all music is sound, isn't it? However without all the small silences between the notes, there would be no music to be heard. It is all the silent spaces between the notes of piece of music that give the music its beauty. Silence in between the notes creates what we call rhythm and melody. So both sound and silence are necessary in the creation of music.

The above analogy demonstrates precisely the same circumstance when it comes to speaking. It is the silences between our words and phrases that infuse meaning into our speeches. It is the silence between words and sentences that creates the all-important rhythm and cadence of speech. We use punctuation to help us remember the necessary silences that give speech its meaning. But sometimes a longer well-placed pause can be so much more than merely silence between words; it can create a sense of drama, suspense, anticipation and even curiosity. Used with skill, a pause is a valued tool in every speaker's toolbox.

Got a Question

One of the most important uses of the pause in any speakers' toolbox, one that is sadly misused by too many speakers, is using the pause to create focus and anticipation just before and then right after you pose a question to your audience. This will add a sense of gravitas to your questions.

Using a pause before a question is a way of letting the audience know that something important is about to happen; because there is a slight break in the flow of your speech, the audience will be curious and they will pay closer attention to what you are saying in order to hear what's coming next. Just before you ask a question, particularly an important or profound question, take a step towards the audience, pause and then ask your question slowly and deliberately. This ensures that they are focusing all of their attention on you. Once you have asked the question pause once again. However this time you are pausing in order to give the audience time to answer the question, because every audience member will always answer a question that you asked whether out loud or in their minds. In fact it is almost impossible not to answer a question that has been posed. For example, what is your favorite colour? See... you started to answer the question.

The more contemplation that is required in the answering of a particular question, the longer the required pause should be. This allows the audience to answer the question in their heads - generally you will pause between two to ten seconds depending on the question. Don't ever step on their answer. In other words, don't ask a question and then just move on with your speech. The audience will still be grappling with their answer to your question and you'll have moved on essentially leaving them behind as you move forward. Always pause long enough to give them the time they need to answer the questions that you have posed.

If you use the "pause – question – pause" technique, you will always connect more deeply. You'll have your audience fully engaged and actively listening and thinking right along with you. You add a whole lot of power to your questions with these types of pauses invariably allowing your questions to pop right out of your speech.

Deep Thoughts

Another crucially important and powerful pause that all speakers must use is the *deep thought pause*. Whenever you say something that is particularly profound, deep in meaning or that you want the audience to pay particular attention to, you must pause to allow them the needed time to process and reflect on what was said and to understand that it was significant. Give them the time to let your words sink in. Again it is a good rule of thumb to also pause just before – the audience will focus more fully on you in anticipation – then give them your pearls of wisdom. Then simply pause again, a little longer than before, as you give them the time to contemplate your wise words. Remember that everything you say, the audience is hearing for the first time and so they need the appropriate time to process your words and concepts and the greater and more complex the concepts the longer they will need to do so.

Never Step on Laughter

Humour, as has often been said with tongue in cheek, is no laughing matter. It is such a hugely significant component of any great speech or presentation that it should never be avoided, over looked or taken for granted. No matter what the occasion, wherever and to whomever you are speaking, there is almost always room for some tasteful well-timed humour.

Many would say the more humour, the better the speech, although that might not always be the case. Remember that while you're giving a speech, you're a public speaker not a stand-up comic. There is a not so slight difference. Humour is such an important element of public speaking that there is a popular saying in the speaking world that "if you want to get paid as a speaker, you'd better make'em laugh".

Humour can be one of the trickiest things to deliver really well. People spend a lot of time and money working hard to get their timing and delivery of humour just right. One aspect of humour that is relatively easy to do, however, is to use an effective pause. Once you've delivered your punch line or punch word you simply step back and pause and let the laughter roll. This particular pause is both an invitation and the giving of permission to the audience to go ahead and laugh. In essence you're saying, "That was a joke, go ahead and laugh now. Don't hold back".

Keep in mind that the larger the audience is in size the more laughter you'll tend to get. Laughter is contagious so once it has started don't ever step on it. Let the audience laugh as much and for as long as they want. The more they laugh, the more they'll remember you. Try adding a few extra words of humour, another punch line, or a funny facial expression and you can easily extend the laughter and make them go wild. Laughter is the money maker, so cash in as much as you can when it's flowing.

If the laughter is really getting out of control and your time is tight you may have to rein them in just to regain control of the audience. You can raise your hand up above your head to get their attention or simply put the palms of your hands up and make a slowing down motion.

Rhythm, Rate, Pitch and Projection

It is, essentially, a matter of the right management of the voice to express the various emotions—of speaking loudly, softly, or between the two; of high, low, or intermediate pitch; of the various rhythms that suit various subjects. These are the three things—volume of sound, modulation of pitch, and rhythm—that a speaker bears in mind."— Aristotle

Rhythm

Most people would agree that what makes a piece of music catchy is not just a good melody but a really good rhythm. You know the kind that keeps things punchy, popping and moving along with excitement, energy and interest. Likewise a good speech should always have a good rhythm for it to keep moving along with excitement, energy and interest. The internal rhythm of a speech, how it moves, just as in music, must maintain energy and the continued interest of your audience members for the duration of the entire speech. Ideally your speech should be made up of a pleasing variety of sentence lengths and their structure should also be diverse in order to avoid monotony and repetition. Think about it, if every sentence has the exact same rhythm as the one before and the one right after it, you'll be lulling your audiences to sleep. No audience member should ever feel that they are enduring a dull monotonous drone.

I remember, in my second year of university, I had the misfortune of having to endure a weekly lecture with the most boring monotonous professor. She was so bad that it seemed she put all her effort into being dull. I would literally drink two large cups of coffee right before her lecture simply in an effort to stay awake – sadly it didn't always work. Listening to her speak was like taking a fist full of sleeping pills. Her total lack of modulation, every sentence like a bullet point, and most disturbingly, her complete oblivion to the fact that she was communicating complex information, earned her the nickname "The Sleeper". I learned a lot about speaking from her - incidentally, not her field of expertise.

As you can see, a speech's rhythm is just as important as your vocal variety. Both are needed for your speech to have musicality. When all your sentences sound the same, your speech can easily end up sounding like a wearisome laundry list being read out loud, point by point, with no progression or direction. When you infuse varied rhythm to your speech it instils energy and interest into your entire presentation; it creates a strong momentum, a clear direction, a sense of purpose and musicality.

When you are writing out your speech, always consider the internal rhythm that you're creating. Do your sentences and words flow together? Are they varied and interesting and leading with momentum toward a clear purpose? Remember that in a speech its best to use longer sentences sparingly. This is not a hard and fast rule though longer and more complicated sentences do require a greater degree of focus and attention from your audience members. Rather you should favour shorter, tighter and more direct sentences. Short direct sentences are considerably easier to listen to, follow, and understand. When writing, it's common to use some longer more complicated sentences and fancier language. Remember reading is different from hearing. When information is spoken out loud, as opposed to read in your mind, the spoken words must first be heard, then deciphered into language and finally understood. So think of those short simple direct sentences, the ones that we typically use in regular conversation, as the easiest way to be understood when heard.

When delivering a speech, strive for a natural conversational flow, spoken in familiar words, and unencumbered by complicated sentence structure because your job is to ensure that your message gets across to the entire audience, not just those with a high level of literacy or an extensive vocabulary. The next time you hear a conversation between two friends pay attention to the flow and rhythm of their speech - that is what you are striving for – the natural easy rhythm of a conversational. As the great professional speaking instructor, Patricia Fripp, would say, "A speech is not a conversation but it should always be conversational"[18].

Rate

The average English speaker speaks at a rate of about one hundred to one hundred and fifty words per minute[19]. As a presenter you want to keep yourself at the lower end of that scale. You'll be hard to understand and follow if you speak too fast. A clear, deliberate, and well-paced speech is key to being fully understood. Keep in mind that as you speak your own words, your brain has already done all the processing work and you know their intended meaning and their expressed implications. You are the master of your sentences and the concepts to which you are giving

---

[18] Fripp, P. (2017). A Good Speech Is Like a Good Conversation. Retrieved from https://www.fripp.com/a-good-speech-is-like-a-good-conversation/

[19] Williams, J. R. (1998). Guidelines for the use of multimedia in Instruction. *Proceedings of the Human Factors in Ergonomics Society Annual Meeting, 42*(20), 1447-1451.

voice. However from the point of view of a listening audience things are different. Your audience must first decode the sounds they hear into words, and then they must understand those words as sentences and ultimately derive the meaning of those concepts. Listening to a speaker and understanding what they are saying takes time when the received information is new or somewhat complicated. So keep in mind that an audience member must listen to and also process all the information that is given at virtually the same time that it is heard. You can see how this becomes more and more important the longer the speech. The audience takes a longer time and requires more decoding work than you the speaker who is merely repeating what they have already processed and prepared. Remember that listening always takes more time and effort, so don't speak too fast.

If you speak too fast, especially when delivering a longer speech, your audience will likely struggle to keep up with your train of thought. They miss a few crucial words here and there and as a result they fail to understand your concepts as intended. The simple answer is to slow down and speak clearly paying particular attention to how you enunciate every word.

If English is not your first language then you must practice speaking any word that you struggle with pronouncing out loud until you get it to come out smoothly. You may simply want to avoid words you find hard to say. Try doing a web search for synonyms that will be easier for you to pronounce so that they are clear when spoken. Most importantly, speak slowly.

Here are some things to consider when it comes to rate:

- Speed up your rate of speaking when you want to add some excitement to what you are saying.
- Slow right down when you want to create a sense of drama and suspense.
- Vary the rate throughout your speech for a more dynamic delivery.

Pitch

Just like variety is said to be the spice of life, you can also add more spice to your presentations by varying your pitch with the effective use of vocal variety. Never ever allow yourself to be a monotone speaker when addressing an audience. So much meaning is conveyed through the tone of your voice. Think of all those times in the past when you suffered through drab and boring monotone speakers, your eyes glazing over, yawning and eventually begging for a quick and painless death. Okay so I'm being a bit dramatic, but I'll bet that you know exactly what I'm talking about. A common culprit for a drab and boring speech is being monotone and expressionless.

Once more, using our musical analogy, one can easily understand how music is entirely dependent on the varied use of notes in creating of pleasing and interesting melody. If an entire song was comprised of only one note repeated for the song's entire duration, it would be an exceedingly boring song. The human voice, as your instrument, is much the same. It requires modulation in pitch to create a sense of passion and persuasiveness, to be inspirational or motivational, or to be funny, informative, or entertaining. Tone is everything.

As I've said before, don't let yourself be a boring monotone speaker; there is no excuse for it. Now I'm not suggesting that you sing your entire speech as though you were at a karaoke bar doing your best impersonation in order to get vocal variety. As an effective speaker what you must strive for first and foremost is perfectly clear enunciation. Then add ample expressiveness and melodiousness to your sentences, vary the pitch of your voice all while clearly emphasising your prominent points and key messages. Try play singing a few lines from your speech. Notice how much more articulate and interesting the words and sentences sounds. The pitch goes up and down, the tone varies, and there is variety. Try using this musicality while repeating the same lines in a speaking voice. When done well, you will be adding drama and passion to your words.

Here are few things to consider about pitch:

- A lower deeper pitch is authoritative.
- A higher pitch denotes excitement and action.
- Questions should be loud and clear and sound like a question with a lilt at the end.
- Lowering your voice to a whisper when revealing a "secret" or key point can be a powerful tool for getting the audience to focus on your words, however always make sure that you are always projecting your voice.
- A loud voice will command attention and denote authority and affirmation.

Play around with your pitch to see what works for you and in what circumstances and don't be afraid to use the effects of voice modulation to keep your audiences interested in what you are saying.

Projection

Now that you understand how to use rhythm, rate, and pitch for maximum effect, you must also ensure that your entire audience can hear you no matter where they may be seated. That is precisely where good voice projection comes into play. Personal experience is the best teacher and like me, I'm sure that you have attended speeches, workshops and the like where you struggled to hear what the speaker was saying because of poor projection. Make sure that you are always loud and clear. Obviously you won't be able to communicate anything at all if the audience can't hear what you are saying. Granted sometimes there isn't much that a speaker can do to control technical problems –

for instance if the PA system or microphone isn't working properly in a room that is simply too large to be filled with an unamplified voice – in those instances you just roll with the punches and do your level best to project your voice as much as possible. I advise that you make sure the audience can hear by simply asking them through a show of hands. Believe me; things do sometimes go wrong with equipment so make sure you are prepared to project your voice when necessary.

At times you will be asked to speak in a room that does not have a provided microphone and PA system. If the room is small enough where one isn't really warranted then there is nothing to worry about. Sometimes however you may find yourself in a large room with no provided microphone - for whatever reason – and the show must go on. These instances are precisely the occasions were strong projected voice is absolutely crucial to your speaking success.

A very effective trick that I have developed and that I always use in such situations is to zone in on an audience member in the very back row and to speak to them specifically – of course only in terms of your voice projection. This trick is only for your benefit and you should give absolutely no indication to that person of what you are doing. The benefit of this technique is that it will force you to project your voice to that person in the back of the room, and by implication, to the entire room. If you only focus on and speak to the front row, or worse, if you don't even consider your speaking volume at all, then you and your voice may well end up coming across as week, frail, and inaudible to many in the audience.

Again, and I can't say this enough, variety is that all important needed spice, so you'll want to make sure to add a variety to your speaking volume throughout your presentation, going at times from a whisper to a shout as appropriate, while always making sure that you are projecting your voice to the entire room. Don't overdo it, moderation is the key. The point of projection is to create emphasis as needed and not to replicate a staged melodrama.

Vocal variety will help you make your presentations more dynamic while keeping your audiences engaged and interested for the entire duration of your speech.

Your voice is your most valuable instrument, and like any instrument, what it does is entirely dependent on your mastery of it. Learn, practice and use the above tools to enliven your delivery and to create dynamic and memorable presentations. As you work toward improvement, I strongly recommend that you always record yourself and then watch and listen to your speech critically - preferably a dry run before you deliver it to the intended audience – this will give you the opportunity to tweak and perfect the mastery of your instrument and guarantee the dynamic delivery of your message.

The Stage

"All the world's a stage..." Shakespeare

Have you ever considered the fact that any speech or presentation is essentially both an audio and a visual experience from the point of view of an audience? A big mistake that many would-be speakers make is that they only consider and focus on the audio portion of their speech - the words, sentences and concepts – but are somewhat oblivious to the visual component of their speech. We have already discussed some of these "visual components" but there is one visual tool available to you that you may find surprising.

This powerful tool, definitely one of the most important available to any speaker, is the use of the stage or platform. Long gone are the days of merely standing statically behind a lectern or podium like a politician. Today, stagecraft is much more dynamic and audiences are increasingly expecting it. Unless you are giving a very formal address such as a commencement speech or a eulogy, you should avoid being static at the podium or lectern. You must see the lectern for what it is; a barrier that separates you from your audience. Inexperienced or reticent speakers often use it as an all-too-easy crutch to lean on or simply as a prop to hide behind. Even if you do feel a bit uncomfortable or exposed, it is crucial that you step out from behind the lectern or podium and onto centre stage if you want any sense of dynamic or dramatic delivery. You'll immediately see the difference in how the audience responds. They'll feel much more connected to you and you'll likewise feel much more connected to them. It's a win-win situation.

Twenty years ago it may have been acceptable or even the norm for a speaker to deliver a speech from the podium, however today's presenter has stepped out onto centre stage in a much more engaging way that audiences have increasingly come to demand.

There are several highly effective ways in which a properly planned and focused use of the stage can greatly enhance the quality and delivery of your presentations. Good staging creates the physical corroboration and confirmation of what you are saying by matching your words to your stage movements. Oral communication is always deeper when it is corroborated visually. On a subliminal level, the audience feels the visual confirmation of what they are hearing you say and it makes them feel good.

So let's look at how the stage can be your friend and ally.

A Measuring Stick

The stage can and should be used as a measuring stick to help you physically denote a progression from one extreme to another. From the audience's perspective, the left side of the stage is negative or bad – the further to the left the worse. Conversely, the right side of the stage is good and the further to the right you go, the better it is. So if you were talking about a bad situation that got better, you would start left and walk towards the right while describing the situation to indicate, though your physical movement, a progression from bad to good. The movement must always and only be from left to right if you want to indicate an improvement otherwise the audience will feel that there is something incongruent between your words and your actions. They may not be able to articulate why they feel that way but they will feel incongruence none the less.

Remember that from your perspective or point of view as the speaker, facing the audience, your right is bad whereas your left is good. This physical stage movement holds true for anything that you might be speaking about where you want to demonstrate a contrast, an improvement, or any gradation from bad to good.

It's All About Time

The stage can be used to enhance delivery in other ways too, for instance it can be used to help you denote the passage of time or different points in time. Similar to the above measuring stick technique, a progression from past to present and through to the future can be simply and effectively denoted or delineated by your movements on stage. Again from the audience's perspective, the left side of the stage is always representative of the past; the further to the left, the further in the past; conversely, the right side is representative of the future and the further to the right the further in the future. Consequently the centre of the stage would represent the present period in time. Remember your history books back in elementary school? The historical time scale always indicated the past on the left and the further left the further back in time.

If you need to indicate further in the past or future than the stage allows in terms of space, use the following tool. While standing at the extremity of the stage, simply point to the left or right – depending on which extreme you want to communicate - using your open hand to extend further into the past or the future beyond the limits of the stage. This tool is also useful when you are limited or confined by a small stage or speaking area.

Always remember that from your point of view as the presenter, while you are facing the audience, the above is reversed. This stage tool is a very beneficial tool to get comfortable with and one that will serve you well as you perfect your stage presence.

Staging the Scene

Another very important use of the stage is when you stage the scene. This is when you create and locate a specific scene somewhere precise on the stage. You will want to use this technique liberally when telling stories. As you create a scene with your words, you can simultaneously "pinpoint" the scene at a specific position on stage. The advantage of doing this is that you will thereafter be able to step back into that pinpointed scene and have the audience follow you there; you can even refer to the scene by merely pointing to the pinpointed area of the stage. The audience will immediately know that you are referring to the specific scene that you had "pinpointed" earlier.

You can have several scenes simultaneously pinpointed on your stage during a single speech or presentation. But be mindful not to forget which scene takes place where on the stage because your audiences will feel that something is wrong if you mix up your "pinpointed" scenes. Again they may not be able to identify what is wrong, per se, but they will most likely feel that there is something wrong and incongruent. However if you stage your scene well, the communication will always be deeper as your audience readily pictures the scene as your actions reinforce your message. Later you can re-enter the scene by stepping into the specific "pinpointed" area on stage or even by simply referring to it by pointing.

Staging Points

Whenever you are delivering a speech or presentation that has multiple points, as is often the case, you can assign each point that you are making to a specific area of the stage. This is similar to "pinpointing" a scene as we just saw; however in this instance you are "pinpointing" a particular point.

In the opening part of your speech, when you are providing them with the roadmap to your presentation, you can indicate that, "first we will look at point #1 (assign a place on the stage for the first point), next we will discuss point #2 (moving to your left assign another spot), and lastly we will discuss point #3 (again moving left assigning the last spot on stage)". The advantage of "pinpointing" your speaking points in this way is that, just as we have discussed above, you can easily step back onto and into anyone of your points, or merely point to it with your open hand and the audience will understand what is implied. If you have successfully pinpointed your points on stage, the audience will have correlated each of your speech points to the physical points ascribed to them on stage.

While transitioning from one point to another, you will only need to take a few steps to the next point on the stage and the audience will immediately understand. Your action informs them that you have transitioned from one point to another. Again this creates a deeper level of communication through the use of non-verbal tools that synchronise and reaffirm your words.

Place of Power

At that crucial moment when you are on stage and delivering your "magic", be it your main point, your tip, a secret, or message, you'll want to do so from a position of power. On the platform or stage the position of power is usually at centre-stage and as close to the audience as you can get without making them uncomfortable. Centre-stage is the ultimate place of power on the platform and so it always makes sense to start and end your presentation or speech from this same place of power. Doing so will reinforce your authority and credibility to the audience members before you have even begun to speak to them. Visually you are at the point of focus at centre-stage and therefore commanding of the entire room. Look at news conferences, public addresses - political or otherwise - and even comics in a nightclub or theatre, they all start and end their presentations from centre-stage.

Even though centre stage is the ultimate place of power on the platform, if you are in the middle of telling a story at either end of the stage and you now want to make a strong point or present your message, you can literally step out of your story space by taking a step or two sideways and a step or two closer to your audience, stop, plant your feet and deliver your "magic". In doing so, you will have created a place of power wherever you happen to be on stage. Besides on a large stage it isn't always practical to get to the exact middle of the stage, and so in those instances, anywhere on stage can be your place of power. Just make sure that you differentiate your place of power from your story space by stepping out of the story and into the point.

When you enter that place of power on stage – whether in the middle or just outside your story space - stand still, feet firmly planted and standing erect, so that as you stand still your words will move the audience instead. Your audiences will know that something important is happening when you stop the action and pause and they will listen more attentively to make sure they get your point.

Setbacks and Moving Forward

At this point you understand why you should be using the entire stage when telling your stories or making your points. Another stagecraft technique relates to discussing a personal or professional setback - whether yours, a character's or even an institution's. This is done by simply mirroring your words by physically stepping backwards on stage while facing the audience. As you can see, you can use the depth of the stage as another type of measuring stick. If you are receiving actual or figurative blows, setbacks, or failures in a story you are telling, again you can move deeper back using the depth of the stage to help the audience feel and identify with those setbacks. To the audience you will seem more and more inconsequential as you step further and further back on stage. But don't turn your back to the audience as you move back, you must reverse. Turning your back on the audience is an absolute *faux-pas* and is considered very rude.

The reverse movement, moving forward on stage, represents the accomplishing of goals and milestones, recovering or gaining something. Move forward toward the edge of the stage and the audience will be sure to see what you are saying.

The edge of the stage is the where you will connect the most profoundly with your audience because you are literally closing the gap or the space that separate you from them. The less physical space there is separating you from the audience, the less emotional space they will feel is likewise separating you from them. Since the strongest connection you can establish with an audience is always an emotional connection, this is a worthy point to heed and apply.

You can even, where and when it is appropriate, leave the stage entirely and walk among the audience members and you'll see how the interconnection between you and them will be even stronger. However remember that as you go deeper into the audience, you will also invariably be turning your back on some. Make sure that you continue to make eye contact with the entire audience by periodically turning around to acknowledge them. Practice this beforehand as it can be a bit tricky and remember that this is not always appropriate to the severity or gravitas of certain topics or types of speeches. Makes sure you have planned how you will be getting on and off the stage as well as the course you will follow on the floor. Speak to the organizers, colleagues or friends if you are unsure whether it is appropriate to venture out into your specific audience.

Moving with Purpose

Before we exit from the subject of the stage and stage movement, we must first discuss the most important stage rule – **only ever move with clear purpose.** If you have no reason to move, then don't, rather just stay put. It is much better to be firmly planted to one spot than it is to shuffle or wander aimlessly about the stage. From the audience's point of view, aimless movement can be very distracting as it robs them of their ability to fully concentrate on what you are saying. We've all seen speakers who wander the stage without purpose, whether they are shuffling back and forth like a boxer waiting for a fight, crossing their legs into a weird unbalanced posture, or performing some sort of mini square dance of nervousness. It is very distracting for audiences and will always take away from and weaken the delivery of your message.

The solution to aimlessness is to simply plant your feet shoulder width apart and stay put right where you are until you have a decided reason to move. Unless your planned stage movement is going to add something specific and meaningful to your words, actions and to your stories, it is at all times preferable to stay put where you are on stage while relying on your hand gestures and eye contact to help you connect and communicate.

When I was a kid, my mom would often admonish me saying, "For God's sake Philippe would you please stop fidgeting and stand up straight. How is anyone ever going to take you seriously if you keep moving like a monkey". A lot of time has passed since I was a kid but her words still ring true today as they did back then. Let's face it, fidgeting or aimless wandering are the unintended bi-products of discomfort, nervousness, and a lack of confidence. It's completely understandable and absolutely forgivable to feel some nervousness when on stage addressing an audience - you wouldn't be the first by a long stretch - but you must always do your level best not to appear nervous. That perception will always make your credibility as a speaker suffer. Don't worry too much about using the entire stage if you are feeling tenuous or nervous, as I said earlier, it is much more preferable to stand still and let your eyes and hand gestures take care of all your non-verbal communication. If this describes you, be reserved and use the stage sparingly perhaps to simply transition from one point to the next. In doing so, you'll hide any signs of nervousness that you may be feeling, and you'll come across as more controlled. With time you'll get more and more comfortable and confident with your stage presence as you slowly and systematically start to incorporate more and more of the above mentioned techniques into your delivery.

Use the Entire Stage

Make sure to use the entire stage throughout your presentation. A speaker will often favour one side of the stage as opposed to the other, if you do, your audiences will internalize and personalize the neglect and they will resent you for denying them equal time and attention. Therefore it's important to balance your stage presence by making sure that you pay equal attention. Of course as mentioned above, only if and when you feel comfort and confidence being in front of a live audience. Remember that everything you do and everything that you say is for the sole benefit of your audience, so the deeper the connection you establish, the deeper the level of possible communication.

A thoroughly thought out and perfectly planned use of the entire stage, using the above techniques, goes a very long way towards supporting and reinforcing your message. Don't leave your delivery to chance, you must plan your stage movements with as much care and consideration as given to the preparing of your words, sentences and message. After all, as I hope I have demonstrated, audio and visual work hand in hand.

In so many ways, when it comes to effective stage movements, the audience merely feels the "rightness" of your physical movements in a tacit and intuitive sense. They may not even be cognitively aware of what you are doing and that's not such a bad thing because if the movement isn't smooth or well correlated to your words, the audience will soon notice that something is off. When your words, hand gestures and stage movements are all connected, choreographed, and congruent, a much deeper level of understanding ensues, coupled with profound emotional connection. That, simply put, is your prime objective.

So plan your stage movements carefully to maximize their use and effectiveness. Now that you know all the various ways you can maximize the employment of the stage, it's time to apply them. From "pinpointing" a scene in a story you are recounting, using the stage as a measuring stick, focussing your speaking points with smooth transitions from one to the other, or indicating your successes and setbacks, learn to master the stage as a tool of delivery and you'll be invited back onto it often.

A Few More Words on Delivery

The importance of good delivery can't be underestimated or undersold - it's the "sizzle" in the steak - that special something that brings it all together. When considering the quality of a speech or presentation, it is most often the delivery that really exemplifies the difference between a merely mediocre speaker and a truly polished professional. Superior delivery projects poise, self-confidence and subject matter authority and so it should never be ignored or overlooked. The good news is that no matter what your current comfort level, like all things in life, the more you do something the better you will get at it, so practice, practice, practice and then practice some more! Always remember that preparation saves perspiration.

We have covered a lot so far but there are still many more ways to make your presentations pop. The following are some additional helpful tips, tools and techniques that I routinely use. I know that these will also put some of that "sizzle" into the quality of your delivery.

Be Yourself

It has often been said that the most valuable personal commodity that anyone of us can ever possess is true authenticity . I couldn't agree more and this is particularly true in the world of public speaking. Unfortunately there are more than a few disingenuous speakers out there who try their level best to sound as much as they can like someone else. Maybe they are inspired by and admire the speaking styles of Obama, Les Brown, Tony Robins, or whomever else; they try hard to impersonate their every nuance and gesture believing that it will somehow make them sound better as a result. Sadly, that is never ever the case. This type of imitation is not flattery. It has more to do with personal insecurity – too big a topic to deal with here. But consider this, if you are simply impersonating another speaker, won't you just end up sounding phony, a hollow version of some one more substantial? What would your friends and family think if they heard you impersonating another speaker? They'd probably call you out on it because maybe you don't know who you are but they do. It's worth remembering Oscar Wild's wise witticism when he so poignantly said that, "You might as well be yourself because everyone else is taken"[20] - words worth pondering for a moment.

If you are going to work hard on your style and delivery, or any other aspect of your speaking, spend that time as judiciously as possible and develop your own unique singular voice, your own style, your own unabashed authenticity. That is the highest goal. Get out of your own self-conscious way and simply let your true personality and individuality shine through. You are singular,

---

[20] Oscar Wilde. (1998). *Oscar Wilde's Wit and Wisdom: A Book of Quotations.* Mineola, NY: Dover Publications.

unique, and irreplaceable. When you do find your voice it will be like sunshine breaking through the dark obscuring clouds like a revelation. Be natural.

Your authenticity should shine through your personal stories; especially if you relive them rather than simply retelling them as we have already discussed. Using your natural and individual way of expression, be it your sense of humour, phraseology, your tone of voice or whatever else it is that makes you, you. I find that this naturally happens with time and experience, as it gives rise to our sense of confidence and a comfort in our own voice, but it can be greatly accelerated with focused attention and effort. Always strive to be yourself for it is your single strongest asset. There is only one of you in the entire world so make that uniqueness your prime advantage and stand out in the crowd.

Keep in mind that everything we say and do on stage is somewhat stylized for our purposes. We do it with stories, foundational sentences, and our core messages. While you want to be authentic at all times, do remember to be you in a more polished way. The way you would behave around special company; you tend to sit-up a little straighter, practice better manners, and think carefully before speaking. You are still you, just the better side of you.

A technique that has been very useful to me is imagining that when I'm speaking to an audience I'm actually speaking to a good friend. In doing so I ensure that I am truly being my authentic self. After all, a good friend would easily call you out as a phony if you wandered to far from yourself. Deepak Chopra once said that in all his "...research, the greatest leaders looked inward and were able to tell a good story with authenticity and passion"[21]. It is surely authenticity that, in large part, made them successful leaders in the first place. We see the same in music, art, and every other discipline. The exceptional have found their voice.

---

[21] Goudreau, J. (2011, January 12). Deepak Chopra On Enlightened Leadership. *Forbes*, 1-3.

Record Yourself

I have said it before but it bears repeating; the next time you give a speech, do yourself a huge favour and make sure that you record yourself or have someone else record you. Recording yourself is a must if you want to improve as a speaker.

Your friends and family, who because they love and care about you, often won't dare tell you the hard truth that you really need to hear. They will rarely tell you what to improve in your delivery. Giving feedback isn't easy. In fact the closer the relationship, the harder it is to give an honest critique. They may well feel that there is something that you could be doing better, or maybe there is something you're doing that they find annoying or distracting, the point is that friends and family will often be the most reluctant to give you the truth, the whole truth and nothing but the truth. They don't want to hurt your feelings and will often be the very last to look you in the eye and tell you what they really think about that speech you just delivered.

The same can be said about members of the audience. They too will often hold back their true feelings and impressions, even on the evaluation forms handed out at the end of a workshop or presentation – commonly referred to as the "smile sheet" for that very reason. They call it a "smile sheet" because audiences invariably put a big numerical smiley face on the sheet with five out of five or ten out of ten scores. I'm not suggesting that you're not that good, however, this feedback is not reliable or truly indicative of an audience's true impressions. They mostly want to make you feel good, show their appreciation or they simply want to avoid being perceived negatively. So how are you supposed to know what works and what doesn't work within your speech and its delivery? By far the most effective way is to just record yourself each and every time that you speak.

There is no better way of getting truly objective evidence of what you appear like on stage delivering your speech than by recording it to study later. I'll admit that it can be very tough to look at a video of yourself on stage, especially the first few times you sit down to look at the footage, but I guarantee that it does get easier over time. It's kind of like the first time you hear your recorded voice on an answering machine, your think, is that really what I sound like? Just like the sound of your recorded voice gets easier to hear so will looking at the footage of yourself on stage.

When studying a recording of yourself delivering a speech, look at your hand movements, are they natural? Are you fidgeting? What about your stage movement, are you moving fluidly and with clear purpose? Go through all aspects of your speech, as we have explored together through these pages making detailed notes of your first impressions, making sure to note not only what works but also what could be improved upon. Then you'll be able to focus on something specific to improve on, getting it under control, and then moving on to the next item and repeating the process. Always start with what stood out the most, that thing that was driving you crazy. By doing this, you will slowly and systematically improve your delivery over time. Keep recording and comparing past performances to your new perfected presentations and you'll see objective evidence of your improvement, helping you stay focused and creating forward moving momentum.

Create a Multi-Sensory Experience

The more senses that you can awaken in your audience the more connected they will invariably fell especially when you're recounting stories. Audiences will live your stories more vicariously if you give them multi-sensory tools by including descriptions of sights, sounds, tastes and smells, and how things feel. The kinesthetic, visual and auditory learners in your audience

– in essence everyone - will appreciate your effort. This is exactly what they need from you. They want to "feel", "see" and "hear" your story, so give them the full multi-sensory experience they are craving and you'll have them eating out of the palms of your hands.

Dialogue Between Characters

When telling a story or recounting a tale, characters are often instrumental to its development by moving the story along and giving us more perspective. Providing your characters with dialogue is a sure way to make them come to life, adding drama, be it tragic or comic to your story and therefore to your entire speech. When you allow your characters to speak for themselves through dialogue, the audience hears their voice through you, add a slight physical embodiment of their characteristics – be it short or tall, reserved or easy-going, loud or quite – and your audiences will more vividly imagine and therefore connect more deeply. For instance, rather than saying something like "my boss told me to get it together or he'd fire me", try delivering it like this. When I got to work that morning my boss sat me down in his office, looked me in the eye, and with a methodical voice said, "Phil, I'm really disappointed in you. Listen carefully. If you screw up just one more time, that's it, you're done. Got it?" See how much stronger the dialogue was. If you also impersonated or embodied the boss, you could use that dialogue to create a sense of curiosity, suspense, and drama and with that your message resonates all the louder. Always find a way to insert dialogue into a story, let your characters speak for themselves, as you can see from the example above, it is much more engaging and dramatic to listen to. Be mindful of how you choose to represent a character. You never want to go overboard with the theatrics – it's not Shakespeare - rather you are simply adding some flesh to the bone.

Creating dialogue between two or more characters shouldn't ever feel like a game of Ping-Pong, with the audience bouncing their heads from side to side, as you jump from one spot to the next. In other words, avoid saying something in one character's voice, then taking a few steps, turning around and answering in the voice of the other character. I've seen speakers do this and it drives me crazy. Simply put, it's not natural, it's annoying and distracting to your audience. Here's the trick to doing it right: while facing the audience, stand in one spot and then tilt your body to the right when speaking as one character and then simply tilt to the left when responding. There is no need for you to step. All you need to do is adjust your stance slightly while standing in one spot. The audience will understand that there is a dialogue between two characters.

Keep it simple. The fact of the matter, subtlety hinting at a character is usually more than enough. Change your voice and your demeanour and the audience will easily imagine the rest. In taking on the character, modify your posture, change the tone of your voice, take on a different accent or any aspect of the character's persona that is informs who they are and what they are like - just don't overdo it. Remember, all you need to give the audience is a subtle hint and they'll do the rest.

Another very effective way to differentiate between characters is when a character says the name of the person they are addressing as part of the dialogue. For example you might say something like this: she looked at me and said "Phil you've got to be kidding me", "Betty I assure you that I'm being serious", "Phil I never know when to believe you" You get the idea. By simply identifying the characters by their names, the audience knows which character is speaking and you don't need to add much narration. This allows the dialogue to flow much more naturally and if you have incorporated some of the other tools mentioned above, your stories will really come to life.

You can also have your entire audience be representative of a character in your dialogue. This tool has the added advantage of directly involving the audience in your presentation. Of course, the audience would not be required to respond they'd just be listening to you, but all the same you can have them represent the person that the character is speaking to. Look directly at them when delivering your lines and they will identify themselves as the other character. Again, this is a good way to engage the audience. By having them represent a character in a dialogue, you choose who they are and what message they hear. Think about it strategically and you'll be able to take full advantage of this tool.

You can also make a specific individual member of the audience a character in your dialogue. The remaining audience will experience this connection vicariously. Now depending on the level of involvement required of the audience member, you may want to arrange this with them beforehand, especially if you expect the individual to respond in character, be it with a gesture of some kind or with specific dialogue. I have seen this used expertly to the general amusement of an entire audience. This is a great technique to use as it not only involves the audience but also allows you create a deeper connection with one audience member and as we saw earlier when you connect to one, you connect to them all.

Another very significant potential with dialogue is infusing humour. By putting the punchline of a joke into the mouth of a character, you can get some great laughs that will pepper and punch-up your stories. Exploit misunderstandings, create some distance on touchy subjects, or simply put some silly foolishness into the mouths of characters and you can quickly see the potential for getting some good laughs as a result. Play with and explore the dialogue potential of characters for humorous infusions but remember to steer clear of anything unkind, unsavoury, or too racy.

Audience Involvement

Getting your audiences involved in your presentations is absolutely central to your speaking success. The very reason that you are speaking in the first place is solely for the audience's benefit. The more involved you make them feel, the more connected they will be. We have already discussed the importance of creating a strong connection through every section of this book, because it is so foundational. There are so many opportunities, no matter what type of speech you are delivering, to get the audience involved, what tools you choose will obviously depend on your objectives.

The following are some great ways to get your audiences involved.

Ask Them a Question

No matter which of the following you choose to do, you are involving your audience.

- You can ask them by show of hands
- You can ask them to respond
- You can ask them rhetorically

Discuss and Debrief

This is where you get the audience to turn to their neighbour to either answer, discuss, or debrief something that you have just covered or to answer a question that you have posed. This is a foundational tool for trainers or workshop presenters where the audience is broken into small pods of about four individuals where they work on an activity together and then present the results to the entire group.

- Get your audience to stand up and stretch. This activity is perfect for those kinesthetic learners who need some physical movement to help them get the most from their learning.

- For longer presentations, this activity is perfect for shaking things up and allowing your audiences to re-energize. Typically everyone gets involved and participates in the activity.

- Before you hand over control of your presentation to your audience, set a time limit for the activity and plan a system for bringing them back; clapping your hands, a bell or buzzer, etc… be creative and have fun with it.

Break Down the Wall

- The audience is considered the fourth wall in stage terminology. When trying to create a connection with your audience, don't be afraid to break down the wall that separates. When appropriate, step of the stage and mix and mingle with the audience. If you interact with your audience you intensify the connection they feel.

- If possible, refer to some audience members by name. This will take a little bit of planning before your presentation, but it will position you as an insider, a familiar, someone who knows something about the organization. In addition, the audience will identify with that person vicariously – speak to one, speak to them all.

- When addressing the audience use "You".

- Never point with your finger as it comes across as accusatory, rather use an open hand to indicate.

Props, Flip Charts, and PowerPoint

There are many speaking or presentation occasions where you may want to use additional visual aids to enhance your presentation. Perhaps you want to use something to get a laugh or break tension. I have a rubber chicken that I have used in some of my workshops as a trophy for a participant giving the right answer. It always gets a laugh from the audience and the participant has an interesting experience to relate to his or her coworkers or family members. There are times when props work for you and there are times when they work against you, so plan them well and give them thought beforehand. Simply ask yourself whether this adds or detracts, and why you are choosing to use the prop in the first place - what specifically is your objective.

The Flip Chart, although sometimes considered "old school" is an invaluable tool to any workshop session — especially where lots of interaction and audience participation is wanted or required. The proper and effective use of a flipchart can enhance any workshop however when not used effectively, a flip chart can become distracting, ineffective, and at worst a barrier to better communication.

By far, today's preferred visual aid tool is PowerPoint or some similar program for the creation of a slide presentation. We have come a long way since the days of big clunky acetate projectors. Most boardrooms have projectors and screens build right into the infrastructure of the room making it easy to use. Like so many other things mentioned in this book, planning and having a clear purpose are paramount. We have all suffered through some degree of "death by PowerPoint" and I encourage you think about what didn't work in those situations. Essentially like props and flip charts, the PowerPoint deck can enhance your presentation when used well but it can easily be abused by allowing it to take over and dominate your presentation effectively making you, the presenter, close to redundant. Make sure you don't let this happen to you. You are the presenter or speaker and the prop is only there to facilitate your delivery. If it is competing with you, get rid of it right away. Let's have a closer look at visual aids.

Can I get some Props?

When it comes to the use of props - less is always more – that is unless you're an amateur magician act on the peripheries of the Las Vegas strip. Just a couple of weeks ago I was present at a speech competition where the speaker had the following props: a skirted table, a water bottle, a shoebox, magazines, an electrical cord and two members of the audience – all to be used and abused within a 7 minute speech. I literally felt as though I was at some kitschy amateur magician's hour. It was all just a bit too much and too distracting for the allotted time of seven minutes. I couldn't keep myself from asking, "is this really a speech?" Answering my own rhetorical question was a challenge. Maybe it was technically a speech but it really felt cliché, cheesy and just too gimmicky and looking back on it, none of it helped deliver the message, in fact I found that it detracted and watered down the message. This was a case where less would have been more.

Keep your props and gimmicks to a purposeful minimum. They should only ever be used to enhance your message in some way; they shouldn't be the message nor should your message depend on them too strongly. You, the presenter, should be the star of the presentation not some prop or cheap gimmick, so be mindful and keep it classy.

Here are some things to consider when it comes to props:

- **The prop must be relevant to the message**

If your prop does not, in some way, contribute to the objective of your speech or presentation, leave it out.

- **Make sure the audience can see the prop**

    When speaking in front of a larger audience, ensure that everyone can see the prop clearly. It can be frustrating for those at the back if they can't see what you are referencing. The same can be true for small audiences too. Make sure that everyone can likewise see the prop. Be mindful to hold it up high and long enough for everyone to see it.

- **Use the right number of props**

    Use too many props in your presentation and you risk being perceived as a Vaudevillian, rather than a speaking professional. In most instances, one prop will suffice. Depending on the amount of time you have, the nature of the props, and/or whether the props are related, more may be appropriate. Like spices in a dish, use props to enhance the flavour, not to overpower the dish.

- **Make sure the prop works**

    If your prop is complicated, test it and re-test it beforehand especially if the prop forms an integral part of the presentation.

- **Have a backup in case the prop doesn't work**

    The chances of a simple prop not working are pretty slim but more complicated props can malfunction or even worse not function at all – even if you have tested and re-tested them. So always be prepared to adjust with a well thought out backup plan.

- **Be completely comfortable with the prop**

    You've got to be comfortable handling the prop from start to finish. This includes revealing the prop, handling it, operating it, putting it away and, of course, addressing its purpose.

- **Keep the prop hidden until you need it**

    Granted this is easier with small props. With larger props you may want to try to keep it behind a curtain or in the wings. The advantages to keeping the prop hidden are that it will not distract your audience while you are talking about something else and the prop will have a bigger impact if it is only seen when revealed.

- **Build anticipation before the audience sees it**

    You may want to talk about the prop before revealing it. This will give the prop greater impact when it is revealed. Be careful, this requires the right choreography and the prop needs to live up to the expectation that you create; however, when done well, the effect is powerful.

- **Be creative**

    Be imaginative by thinking of unusual props that will have an impact with your audience. Try finding props that correlate to the metaphors or analogies you are using while making them relevant to your point or message. This is also a good opportunity for some unexpected humour.

- **Put it away when you're done using it**

    Unless you plan to refer to the prop again, it is best to put it away once you are finished using it. Otherwise, the prop will be distracting for the remainder of your presentation.

Flip Charts

Today's world is full of high tech gadgets and gizmos and presenters are becoming more and more reliant on technology when it comes to the use of visual aids. Presenters often feel they must create a presentation using a computer, PowerPoint, and a projector, however sometimes it just isn't practical, feasible, or wanted.

What if you are speaking outdoors? What if neither you nor the organizers have the needed equipment? There are many reasons to go low-tech with a flip chart and many reasons why a flip chart can work more effectively and makes more sense for you to use. Knowing the best practices of using flip charts is a tool that all speakers and presenters must have in their tool kits.

Besides, even though flip charts might be decidedly low tech, they are totally reliable and they require no special technical or computer skills to operate. And lastly, if your projector decides to conk out at the last minute, the simple flip chart can be a welcome hero destined to save the day. A couple of years ago I was booked to speak. I sent my PowerPoint presentation and a list of technical requirements. When I arrived, they were having major issues with the technology. I wrote out all my major points on a flip-chart and it literally saved the day. The point is, you never know when you'll need to rely on flip-charts so get comfortable with them.

Here are a few items to consider when using flip charts:

- Most flip chart stands come with clamps that will hold most types of flip chart paper pads. While most will allow you to hang your flip charts some stands will only allow you to prop them up. Make sure to inquire beforehand and avoid unpleasant surprises.

- If you are brining your own flip chart paper, make sure that the paper pads you plan on using will fit the stand supplied. Some have different spaced holes at the top.

- Flip chart pads are usually sold in packages of two and come either plain or with grid lines printed on them. Lined paper makes it easier to keep your text straight and aligned. Make sure that the pad is perforated at the top for easier tearing way or removal of sheets.

- When preparing your charts, design your charts on paper before drawing them on the actual flip chart pad – this will save precious paper and the final result will look cleaner and neater.

- Lightly write your text in pencil then trace with the actual flip chart markers. This will allow you to make any adjustments with text spacing and any figures you will be drawing. Using upper and lower case letters makes it easier to read and use the 7 x 7 rule. Have no more than 7 words on each line and no more than 7 lines to a sheet.

- Use proper flip chart markers and not regular magic markers. Flip chart markers will not "bleed" through the paper and they don't have a strong toxic smell. In fact you can find "scented" markers. They usually come in various fruit scents.

- Avoid using yellow, pink, or orange. These colours are low contrast and they are extremely difficult for the audience to see. Don't force your audience to squint in order to see your points. Also, avoid using too many colors, one dark color and one accent color works best. If you use too many colours your chart will begin to look psychedelic.

- Prepare some cheat sheets by lightly writing in pencil any notes next to key points you need. The audience won't be able to see them. You may also write a reminder to yourself of what is on the next sheet. Knowing this will allow you to properly introduce your next sheet before flipping over to it.

- Have a blank sheet of paper between each of your text sheets. This will prevent the written material from showing through – the sheets will look clean and clear.

Flip charts can also be used for capturing audience responses, answers, and debriefs. They have a lot of interactive potential. Before introducing a topic, it can be very beneficial to ask the audience to give you their thoughts or ideas on the subject, then throughout your presentation, you have the opportunity to confirm and elaborate on their responses. This can be very affirming and validating for your audiences. Bring tape to hang them up on the walls for reference once you have torn them away from the pad.

For further audience involvement, you may want to ask an audience member to come to the front and be the "scribe". A word of caution, it is always a good rule of thumb to pre-select this individual and make sure they are willing to be the scribe and that they have good penmanship.

Here are a few bonus tips for writing on the chart:

- **Never stand in front of the chart**

    If you are right handed stand with your body to the left of the chart making sure that you are not blocking the view. If you are left handed do the same in reverse.

- **Add an asterisk for spellcheck**

    If you are nervous about your spelling just add an asterisk at the top with the words "spellcheck" and tell the audience that that is your spellcheck in the event of any typos. Do this with humour and they will forgive your mistakes.

- **Always have tape and spare markers**

    Make sure that you always have tape in your presentation kit so that you can tear away sheets and stick them up around the room as references. Likewise, it's a good idea to have spare flip chart markers. You can never tell when they are about to die on you; so be prepared.

PowerPoint and Projection

"People who know what they're talking about don't need PowerPoint" - Steve Jobs

There are lots of strong opinions and many pros and cons attributed to the use of PowerPoint or other projected media in your presentations and you will have to determine for yourself whether it will enhance or confound your message. PowerPoint slides can be very powerful visual tools for presenters and speakers alike. Ultimately it all depends on how they are being used. That is what will determine whether they are either positive or negative.
Most of these programs are incredibly powerful and likewise easy to use and require very little technical knowledge or expertise to master.

Yet we have all experienced death by PowerPoint and we have all been exposed to tedious and torturous presentations as a result. Just because PowerPoint is relatively easy to use, doesn't mean that it is easy to use well and with efficacy. There are certain absolute must do's and best practices that can turn any presentation from tedious to tantalizing, and from torturous to one that creates a tremendous connection.

There is no denying its popularity. PowerPoint is used in boardrooms all around the world. Incredibly, as indispensable as it is to the business world, it is shocking how seldom we feel that a PowerPoint presentation really resonated, where it really hit a home run and knocking it out of the park. Realistically attendees will often oscillate between feeling a mild interest and complete dissatisfaction with a slide presentation.

Some of this can be attributed to the fact that PowerPoint or projected media works better for larger audiences such as Keynotes and TED talk type events. In the boardroom, PowerPoint can sometimes be a hindrance to good constructive discussion and the free engagement in collaborative thinking. If your objective is to have a one-sided presentation of facts, information or to present your results, then the media will work well for you in those instances. However, if your objective is to engage your audience and have them collaborate, then you may want to avoid PowerPoint all together or at least limit its use. The question you must ask yourself is, "will PowerPoint add or detract from my presentation?"

Steve Jobs had a well-known aversion to people using slides in meetings and it was well known inside Apple. "I hate the way people use slide presentations instead of thinking," Jobs told biographer Walter Isaacson. "People would confront a problem by creating a presentation. I wanted them to engage, to hash things out at the table, rather than show a bunch of slides. People who know what they're talking about don't need PowerPoint[22]." Jobs preferred to use the whiteboard to explain his ideas and hash things out with people in the boardroom. The point, although extreme, is well taken.

This doesn't have to be the case for you. Jobs had a certain style and demanded that everyone conform to it. Whether PowerPoint is a good or a bad thing is really up to you and how you choose to use it. Nevertheless Jobs' perspective is good to keep in mind and we should always question the reasons for our actions.

Quintessential to the corporate world, PowerPoint plays no less of a central role in the world of workshops, seminars and adult learning and education; and increasingly, elementary and high school children are being asked to learn and use PowerPoint for their presentations and projects. Its power, purpose and uses are really only limited by your creativity and imagination. As we discussed earlier, audience members tend to have a preferred learning style – kinesthetic, auditory or visual – so as you can see projected presentation slides are perfect for visual learners and will enhance their experience.

If you haven't yet, in all likelihood, you will at some point in time need to use this technology, so here are a few key points to consider if you want to make your projected presentations sparkle.

---

[22] Isaacson, W. (2011). *Walter Isaacson Great Innovators e-book boxed set.* New York, NY: Simon & Schuster.

Keep it Simple

- The slides are not the "star of the show". People came to hear you and to be moved or informed by you and your message. Don't let it get derailed with slides that are unnecessarily complicated, busy, or full of what Edward Tufte calls "chart junk"[23]. Nothing in your slide should ever be superfluous.
- Your slides should have plenty of "white or negative space." The less clutter you have on your slide, the more powerful your visual message will be.

Limit bullet points & the amount of text

- Less is more – with the exception of font size.
- The best slides have little to no text at all.
- Try just using a great graphic or telling photograph; after all, isn't a picture worth a thousand words?
- No more than 6 words per slide. Instead of a bullet, go to a new slide
- Your slide should only be a cue or prompter for you to elaborate on. Keep the information on the slide to a minimum.

Limit transitions & animation

- Don't overuse animations and slide transitions - that means rarely.
- Avoid anything that is too busy, bouncy, or over the top. Keep it professional, clean, and sedate.

Use high-quality graphics

- Only use high-quality graphics and photographs. If you get them online be cognisant of copyright issues.

---

[23] Tufte, E. (1983). *The Visual Display of Quantitative Information*. Cheshire, CT: Graphics Press.

- Avoid using PowerPoint Clip Art or other cartoonish line art; don't undermine your professionalism with junk.

Have a visual theme, but avoid using PowerPoint templates

- You must have a consistent visual theme throughout your presentation, but most templates included in PowerPoint have been seen by your audience countless times. They don't need to see it again.
- Your audience expects a unique presentation with new (at least to them) content, avoid cookie-cutter presentations.
- You can make your own background templates. You can also purchase professional templates on-line (for example: www.powerpointtemplatespro.com).

Use appropriate charts

- Always ask, "How much detail do I really need?" Presenters are often guilty of including too much data.

Pie Charts

- Used to show percentages. Limit the slices to 4-6 and contrast the most important slice with color or by exploding the slice.

Vertical Bar Charts

- Used to show changes in quantity over time. Best if you limit the bars to 4-8.

Horizontal Bar Charts

- Used to compare quantities. For example, comparing sales figures among the four regions of the company.

Line Charts

- Used to demonstrate trends.

Using Colour

- The right color can help persuade and motivate. Studies show that color usage can increase interest and improve learning comprehension and retention[24].
- Cool colors work best for backgrounds.
  They appear to recede away from us into the background.
- Warm colors generally work best for objects in the foreground.
  They appear to be coming at us.
- When presenting in a dark room use a dark background with white or light text.
- If most of the lights are on then a white background with black or dark text works much better.
- Use strong contrasting colours and avoid yellows, pinks or any light colours.

---

[24] Dzulkifli, M. A., & Mustafar, M. F. (2013). The Influence of Colour on Memory Performance: A Review. *The Malaysian Journal of Medical Sciences : MJMS*, *20*(2), 3–9.

Choosing your fonts

- Use the same font set throughout your entire slide presentation, and use no more than two complementary fonts.
- San-serif fonts are generally best for PowerPoint presentations.
- Make sure the text can be read from the back of the room.

Using video or audio

- Use video clips to show concrete examples. It promotes active cognitive processing, the natural way we learn.
- Using a video clips illustrates your point better and also changes the pace, increasing the interest of your audience.
- Avoid cheesy sound effects.

A few final thoughts on PowerPoint

- Slides are meant to support the speaker – make sure they don't dominate your presentation.
- Never, ever turn your back on the audience and read text from the slides word for word. This is the greatest presentation sin.
- Don't squeeze too much information in; audiences are much better served receiving a detailed, written handout as a takeaway.
- Make sure your slides have a natural and logical flow. Don't be afraid to re-arrange them if necessary.
- Don't hand out print-outs of your slides. They don't work without you there.
- Go to "Black Screen" by typing "B" on your keyboard when you want the audience to focus on you rather than the slide.
- Practice, practice, and practice your presentation again before your present it.

Nerves

Admittedly the greatest hurtle or barrier in delivering a good speech is simply fear. Fear is a barrier of our own construction and only we can overcome it. It comes when you feel a lack of control, stress or anxiety. Fear can be crippling if you let it. It can rob you of opportunities as you talk yourself out of doing the things you want to do.

If you happen to feel this way, take courage in the fact that you are not alone and there are things you can do that will help. As I said at the outset of this book, the fear of public speaking is one of the most prevalent and common phobias in the world and one most that of us have to a certain extent. The fear of public speaking is closely related to performance anxiety. We are all concerned about how we are perceived, about appearances and the judgements that follow. Nobody wants to appear anxious in front of an audience. Sweaty pits, hands and forehead, a parched mouth, stuttering over words, uncontrolled nervous shaking or God forbid a complete panic attack, the fear is real. Unfortunately, there are no easy solutions, no simple pill that you can swallow as a cure, it simply comes down to doing everything you can to be as fully prepared as possible.

Anxiety can be overcome, your fears can be surmounted, and you can be as cool as a cucumber on that stage facing your audience. I have been privileged to see it firsthand countless times. You too can overcome your fears, whatever they may be.

After presenting the eulogy at my father's funeral, I knew that I needed to improve my public speaking abilities, as the result of some persistent coaxing from some colleagues, I eventually joined a workplace Toastmasters club. When I first joined the group, I was practically paralyzed with fear and felt way outside of my comfort zone and I felt the butterflies fluttering in my belly. But over time and with an awful lot of practice, by putting myself out there, I was finally able to get those butterflies to fly in full formation supporting and energizing me as I spoke. Systematically my nervousness lessened and is no longer a hindrance to my speaking; in fact it eventually became the very source of energy that I needed in order to give a great dynamic and impassioned performance.

If you have never heard of Toastmasters then I urge you to look them up right now. Explore what they offer and how they can help you. Chances are there's a club close by that you can easily join, maybe there's one where you work, and believe me, you won't regret joining. Another great public speaking organization you should consider is The Dale Carnegie Public Speaking Program. I know many successful speakers who have graduated from this excellent program who have much to say about its efficacy. Incidentally, Warren Buffet only hangs one of the countless certificates and diplomas he has earned and been honoured with throughout the course of his long life – and yes you guessed it; he has only hung his Dale Carnegie Certificate. That in itself speaks volumes about the importance of good public speaking.

The most important aspect of the above public speaking organizations is that they give you ample stage time to practice, polish, and perfect your speaking skills. In addition, you'll get invaluable feedback from your fellows that, once applied to your future speeches, will surely help you further improve your skills all the while mitigating your anxiety level. Feedback is indispensable to growth.

That being said, to me, the best tool for getting over your fear of public speaking is to be completely and totally prepared. As I am fond of saying, "preparation saves perspiration". The fact of the matter is that all too often, a nervous speaker is a speaker who has not sufficiently prepared for the task at hand and they know it and they feel it so of course they are nervous. I would be too. So much of that anxiety simply arises from a lack of preparation. By understanding the three pillars of public speaking - content, structure and delivery – and being sufficiently prepared, a polished presentation will surely ensue. Great content is not enough. The content needs a proper structure, while delivery puts that "sizzling" irresistibility into your performance.

Practice your speech over and over again; practice it while standing in front of the mirror; create the conditions of the event as best you can; and use your full projected voice and you will gain the confidence you need. With each rehearsal, visualize yourself on that stage successfully delivering your speech to an elated and appreciative audience. Pay particular attention to those rough areas that you find challenging until they are smooth.

Remember when you were back at school faced with a quiz, a test or an examination? Isn't it true that whenever you felt prepared – when you had studied sufficiently – that you preformed much more confidently, successfully and felt less anxiousness? Well the very same is true when it comes to public speaking – the better and more prepared you are the better and more polished you will be. Again, preparation saves perspiration.

Practicing by yourself is important but it might not be enough for you to alleviate your fears. Here are a few suggestions for controlling your nerves and lessening your anxiety. While what works for each individual may vary greatly, my hope is that one or more of the tips, tools, and techniques listed below will work for you.

- **10 to 15 minutes before you speak, focus on your breath.** Breathe deeply and evenly relaxing your body and relieving tension.

- **Drink lots of water and have a glass or bottle with you on stage.** If you feel parched, take a pause, have a sip and then continue.

- **Practice your speech as many times as it takes.** Run through your speech until you've got it polished and you feel confident.

- **Focus on the material not the audience.** By focusing on your well-rehearsed material as opposed to the audience, you will feel a greater sense of control.

- **Arrive early.** Giving yourself plenty of time to ensure your equipment works and that everything is ready will allow you to relax.

- **If you are reading your speech.** Always keep your finger on the line and word you are reading so you don't lose your place.

- **If you tend to sweat.** Be prepared by having a napkin and wearing clothes that won't reveal sweat marks

- **Get a good night's rest.** Increase your sense of relaxation by going to bed early the night before. Your mind will be clearer.

- **Exercise to relieve tension.** Physical activity is a sure way of releasing some of the anxious energy that can build up. Just don't overdo it.

- **Have a good meal.** Make sure that you have the nutrition to give you energy on stage, however never eat less than an hour before you speak.

- **Don't be afraid of silence.** If you get lost in your speech, take a pause, breathe deeply until you regain your composure – usually this will happen within just a few seconds.

In my experience, and I've seen this happen more times that I can count, audiences are always rallying for the speaker, especially when things seem to be going wrong. They might be mortified for you but they always want you to succeed. Give it a moment's thought and you'll soon recognise that you would feel the same way. We all have empathy and compassion. It is a very rare occasion indeed when an audience member lacks this innate sense of generosity. So next time you feel a bit nervous, remember that your audience members want you to succeed, so let the pressure go, and let yourself feel that you are flying with a safety net.

A Few Final Words

Speaking with eloquence and poise really is one of the most important skills that you can develop for your career and personal life that will pay dividends over and over again throughout the course of your life. Too often, people miss opportunities or are overlooked in their careers because they either have no confidence or they have no knowledge and skill in public speaking. Is your career suffering or stagnant?

Sometimes it is a special occasion that has come and gone, a missed opportunity, or a chance to share your thoughts. We often end up beating and berating ourselves for being reluctant or scared. We miss opportunities to share a few words in praise, thanks, or congratulations only to beat ourselves mercilessly on the way home. I can think of many times when that was the case for me.

Our voice expresses our deepest thoughts, passions, and concerns; it enlivens, enlightens, or entertains; it educates, elucidates or informs the world; it is by far our most powerful gift and one that we must learn to master.

My hope is that the three pillars of this book – Content, Structure and Delivery – have made it easy to understand the principles behind successful public speaking and that the tips, tools and techniques that I have given will give you some insight into how to put it all into practice. As they say, Rome wasn't built in a day. Likewise you too will become a great speaker if you consistently and systematically practice, practice, and practice some more. If you commit yourself to the process you will reap the rewards and public speaking will become more and more effortless. Only a true commitment to improving, perseverance in excellence, and tenacity in the face of difficulties can bring you to your ultimate and complete success. Keep in mind that as with all things, the more you put in the more you get back. What will you get out of this book is up to you and what you put in. Only you can determine what your successes will be.

When I decided to commit to public speaking excellence, I sought and accepted every single speaking opportunity available. If there was an audience, I was ready to speak whether to five or five hundred, it made no difference. I was hungry. I always asked for detailed feedback wherever I could, I videotaped every single speech that I delivered, and I sought the guidance and mentorship of all those who could teach, coach and inspire me. By immersing myself fully into the world of speaking, in essence by walking the talk, I got better and better over time. The better I got the more sought after I became. To this day, I still do everything I can to constantly improve every aspect of speaking in public.

If only I had had this book when I was starting out - What a difference it would have made; how much faster I could have progressed; how many silly mistakes I could have avoided. As they say hindsight is 20/20. I wrote this book for YOU. I want you to avoid the time and effort I spent wandering and lost in the proverbial dessert. With this book your time will be greatly reduced, your speaking success will be more focused and expeditious, and your confidence and the assurance that you are doing the right thing would have arrived a whole lot sooner.

Over the past several years, I have been repeatedly approached by many would be speakers, looking for advice and guidance on the art of public speaking. I realized that there was a need for guidance that was not being sufficiently met. Consequently, I created many workshops and seminars, gave countless speeches on the subject, and had numerous one on one consultations. It became the genesis of this book and provided me with much of the material for this book.

My simple and humble goal in writing this book is to give the reader real and tangible tips, tools and techniques that I have discovered and developed right there on the stage; tools that have brought me continued success and many accolades, and that I am honoured to share with you and all the other would be speakers in the world. This book will help you achieve your own many successes on the platform.

Every important aspect of speaking and presenting has been touched upon within these preceding pages. However that being said, no single book could ever encapsulate the enormity of this subject. My simple goal is to make the reader aware of the many different aspects that must be considered in the preparation and presentation of a good speech. Only you can make it a great speech with your authenticity, your passion, and most importantly of all, with your patient and persistent practice.

I wish you every speaking success for you next engagement, whatever it might be, and every one that follows. I am confident that if you apply the lessons of this book in earnest with a commitment to excellence, you will indeed razzle and dazzle your audience and have them begging for more. I know you can do it, I hope you do too.

Appendix

In this section you will find invaluable survival tools for your next speaking gig. These easy to use guides are designed to provide you with just enough information to put together your next speech in a pinch. So if you don't have time to read through this entire book right now, simply find the type of speech you need to deliver and follow the easy steps and instructions and you'll have a speech in hand and ready to deliver in no time at all. Once you have your speech prepared, I strongly recommend that you read the portions of this book that relate to your speech, its audience, and your desired outcome. Of course, the best possible course of action for the best possible results is to read this book in its entirety as much will be overlooked otherwise.

Many of the speeches included below are "special" or "social occasion" speeches or as the Ancient Greeks called them - Epideictic Speeches. Take comfort in the fact that you are adding to a long line of historical figures. The preparation and delivery of special occasion speeches can be traced all the way back to at least the Ancient Greeks and in all likelihood much further back into our common collective past.

I have also included references to some relevant page numbers to the various parts of the book that you should review as you put your speech together. These references will help you add a bit more panache to the final product and they will likewise give you some guidance to the most important aspects to consider -aspects that will make your speech and its delivery shine just a bit more brightly.

Once you have your speech ready, you must practice it until its right, no matter how many times are required in order for that to happen – remember preparation saves perspiration.

Speech of Introduction

A speech of introduction is a short speech that introduces the main speaker at an occasion and should inspire the audience to pay attention to that speaker. It is important to enhance the speaker's credibility. Try to meet them in person, by email, or on the phone and always make sure to do your homework and that the information is accurate.

A speech of introduction should always be brief and to the point although the brevity might depend on how familiar the audience is with the speaker's topic. If they are not familiar, then you will want to elaborate. There are three components to keep in mind:

- You must provide a brief backdrop or background.

- Introduce the speaker's topic and explain if necessary.

- Invite the audience to warmly welcome the speaker.

Sample:

Our keynote speaker today is someone many of us know and admire. _____ is a leader – not just in the field of small business development – but also in his community helping immigrant entrepreneurs successfully launch their own new business ventures.
The author of two bestselling books on business and of countless articles and blogs, _____ is a true leader in his field. We are privileged today to hear him speak about how he overcame obstacles as a new immigrant and became the successful business leader s/he is today.
Ladies and gentlemen, please put your hands together and give a warm welcome to _____.

The Toast

A toast is a brief tribute to a person or event that also allows the speaker to acknowledge accomplishments and express best wishes for the future. Besides being brief (about 30 to 60 seconds), it should be delivered at a time when everyone is present, perhaps seated for a dinner or when everyone has a drink in hand.

A little preparation and practice can help make the event more enjoyable and memorable. Having in mind one or two things that set the person or event apart is an effective strategy, as well as keeping a positive tone and staying brief. It is advised that you practice in front of a mirror or in front of a friend to become more comfortable with the toast.

- Be positive and uplifting

- Always be sober when delivering the toast

- When in doubt, leave it out. Don't embarrass anyone

- Try your best to come across as spontaneous

- Deliver the words in a conversational, informal manner

- A thoughtful and appropriate poem can work

Sample:

Ladies and gentlemen, please stand and raise your glass.
To _____, a true friend and esteemed colleague to us all, who is so often the first to offer help to those in need; who always strives to be positive and supportive; whose smile is broad and contagious; and without whom, this company would fall apart. On behalf of all of us at_____, please accept our heartfelt gratitude and sincere appreciation.

The Roast

If an individual is leaving a company or an organization or perhaps they have achieved some noteworthy success, they may become the subject of a roast - a roast a humorous toast that pokes a bit of fun in a friendly way. It's considered an honor to be roasted, and generally a roast is reserved for individuals who have achieved respect and a notable reputation.

- Use tributes, admiration, comedic insults, and outlandish stories - true or false – to poke fun.

- The roast master serves as the master of ceremonies while others may also partake in the roasting.

- Often those involved in the roasting might be expected to bear the brunt of a few of the jokes themselves.

- The roastee always deserves very careful consideration, make sure they can take a joke and show good humor and tread lightly.

Regardless of the humorous lighthearted insults used, never lose sight of the objective and ultimate goal of a roast; you are ultimately paying tribute to the person being honored by the good natured fun and humour of a roast. Remember to only use appropriate tasteful humor.

Speech to Present an Award

A presentational speech bestowing an award should give recognition to the recipient and their accomplishments with concern to the specific award being presented. While these speeches might vary in length and content, they should all contain a few key elements.

- Highlight the merits of the award recipient

- Emphasize the purpose and significance of the award being given

- Personalize the speech to make the award and event more meaningful for the recipient and the audience.

- If the recipient is known to everyone, mention the name right away. If it's a surprise, hold off mentioning the name until the end

- The attention should be on the recipient not on the one awarding.

- Hold the award in your left hand and use your right hand to shake the recipient's hand.

Here is an example of a presentational speech:

Our next award is the Top Salesperson of the Year Award, which goes to (drumroll please)... Mary Smith. Mary has consistently crushed her sales targets and gone well above and beyond the average while providing the best possible service her clients. She has undoubtedly earned this honor by being the first in and last out of the office almost every single day. Mary has consistently followed every lead that came her way, she has made herself available to her clients and yet she has still somehow managed to make time to chair our social committee. Mary, we are in awe of your commitment, tireless energy and outstanding results. Ladies and Gentlemen, I proudly present to you this year's Top Salesperson of the Year, Mary Smith.

The Acceptance Speech

The presentation of an award is usually followed by an acceptance speech, which the recipient delivers upon immediate receipt of the award. This speech gives the recipient an opportunity to show appreciation for the award as well as humility and grace.

- Should be prepared ahead of time, if possible

- Expresses sincere appreciation

- Acknowledge and thank those who contributed or had an impact on the success

- Indicate how the award will make a difference to you in your future

Here is Mary Smith's acceptance speech:

Thank you very much for presenting me with Top Salesperson of the Year Award. I want to thank Management for supporting me in my achievement and my fellow sales staff for their continued encouragement. Most of all, I especially want to thank Jack for his invaluable mentorship, his unyielding belief in my sales abilities and for being my go to person when I struggled. Lastly, I want to acknowledge that I am part of a tremendous team of dedicated and hardworking salespeople without whom I could not have had the success I have had – you really do bring out the best in me. I will forever remember this honor, especially on those tough days that we must all face, and I will strive to continue to be deserving of the honour. I want to thank you all once again for this incredible tribute.
Thank you, thank you, and thank you.

The Keynote Address

A keynote address is a speech that often represents the central theme at a convention, conference, or other large assembly summarizing the fundamental message and revolving around the theme. For example, organizers of a conference with the theme of "Visionary Leaders" might want the keynote speaker to celebrate the leaders of that organization, recounting some of the accomplishments that have resulted from their visions thereby inviting audience members to realize, embrace, and be inspired by the importance of being a visionary leader. A Keynote should inspire and motivate the audience to adopt a higher ideal always incorporating a strong call to action as a take away message.

- The keynote speaker always should incorporate the theme of the conference in some way

- The duration of a Keynote can vary from 30 minutes to one hour so preparation is essential to your success

- The typical Keynote might allude to such topics as organizational growth, team building, goals and aspirations, leadership, change, or achievements

- The Keynote speaker is often a person who has earned a reputation within their professional field through expertise or fame

Contact
Phil Tasci

To book Phil for your next event please send email to
info@philtasci.com

You can connect with Phil on social media

For cool stuff and free resources
Visit:

www.SpeakLikeAProTheBook.com

www.philtasci.com

Acknowledgment

The completion of this book is the fulfillment of a long held dream to publish a book and be its author. This dream was shared by friends and family as they encouraged and supported me through the process of its completion. Without them this book would never have been possible. I am indeed indebted.

I want to thank you - my fellow speakers - for buying this book and for reading it. Every connection and experience that we share together makes us better, stronger and more interconnected and so I hope that this book has helped you speak like a pro.

Teachers share their knowledge
Friends share their support
Families share their binding love
We are made of these

About the author

Phil Tasci is an award winning keynote speaker, workshop facilitator and communication consultant with years of experience and expertise in corporate learning and leadership development. Working with both individuals and organizations, Phil specializes in the art of crafting impactful messages, building compelling stories and in helping individuals develop dynamic delivery from the stage.

He lives with his family in Toronto.

NOTES

NOTES

NOTES

NOTES